Religion =

Relationsh

Kindgom = ~~~~ ~~~~ ~~~~ ife

People Condition

Love People = Yes

Grace = Yes

Culture = Yes | open up the door, if God leads

Thinking = "God changes The mind"

Identity = Know who you are!

Be a
★ Presence =

"Racism"

(Life Cycle =

→ Limited = | Mental Illness -
Mental Health

Wisdom = | PSTD -

"Be a blanket to people in Grief

chap 1v
1st

#Compassion #

1. AC Scott
2. Angleaflin -CNA (Hospic funeral)
3. Tangela Black - Brother Stage (4) Florida
   OSCAR JR. DC
4. US - Not Them -Shy-
5.

(Gang-chaplin)   -Root-
                  Spiritual Warefare

The Chaplain's Role

How Clergy can Work with Law Enforcement

By Rev. Terry Morgan, M.Min.P.S., B.C.E.C.R.

DEDICATION

To my wife Phyllis, my son Josh, my daughter Jen, and all of those who have stood side by side with me through thick and thin. This book is dedicated to you.

"The heartfelt counsel of a friend is as sweet as perfume and incense." Proverbs 27:9 NLT

Sheep => 93%

Gauge
Wild Wolf => 4%
Dog   Sheepdog => 3%   - First
                          responder
                          Accident
        HOA => orders,   Purse
                         Snatcher
              Security

Sheepard - 2%

Leadership - Awareness
   Protecting:
        Chaplin

CONTENTS

Acknowledgements   vii
Introduction   x
    SECTION I
    FOUNDATIONAL STRENGTHS CONFOUNDED

Chapter 1. So What's so Special About Being a Cop   3

Chapter 2. The Well Worn Path from Altruism to Cynicism   13

Chapter 3. The Five Major Stresses in Law Enforcement   23

Chapter 4. The Onset of Moral Decay and Cynicism   61

    SECTION II
    COMPROMISE OF CHARACTER

Chapter 5. Like Scarecrows in a Melon Patch   67

Chapter 6. PTSD – Haunted Officers Needing Help   73

Chapter 7. Divorce – Broken Promises   85

Chapter 8. Suicide – The End of a Legacy   91

    SECTION III
    CHARACTER RE-ENFORCED

Chapter 9 Sharpening the Stone   97

Chapter 10 Raising the Shield   103

Chapter 11 Shining the Armor   113

Chapter 12 A Plume for the Helmet   121

SECTION IV
THE CHAPLAIN'S ROLE

Chapter 13. Take my Hand   131

Chapter 14. Marriage Help   147

Chapter 15. Law Enforcement Officers and Suicide   153

Chapter 16. Officer Involved Shootings and Officer Down Calls   161

Other books by this author   174

Appendix A   175

Notes to Section I   177

Notes to Section II   183

Notes to Section III   185

Notes to Section IV   189

Bibliography   193

ACKNOWLEDGMENTS

"For God is not unrighteous to forget your work and labour of love, which ye have shewed toward his name, in that ye have ministered to the saints, and do minister."
Hebrews 6:10

Thank you to Officer Matt Alves of the Lincoln Police Department for the incredible artistic design and work on the book cover. You do awesome work my friend.

Thank you to all of the men and women in law enforcement across the United States and abroad who put their lives on the line in protecting us and keeping us safe. In particular I would like to thank the officers in Sacramento and Placer Counties who have allowed me to participate in their lives and work alongside them as a chaplain and friend. Thank you and God bless you.

Thank you to the Chaplains who have come in and out of my life over the years. Thank you Chaplain Andrea for your brilliant editing.

Thank you to the Chaplains and Board of Directors of Gold Country Chaplaincy. You have been incredible.

Last but not least I want to say thank you to my family and friends: my loving wife Phyllis; my great kids Josh and Jen, and all the chaplains who have served alongside me. You have all encouraged me more than you know. You have helped me to stretch beyond my comfort level and be all that God has for me.

Thank you all and God bless you all.

THE CHAPLAIN'S ROLE

INTRODUCTION

A Chaplain is generally a clergy person with specialized training dealing with people in areas of grief and trauma, and within their specific field or industry i.e. hospitals, military, law enforcement, etc. Pastors and other ministers that work in this field are traditionally given the title "chaplain", and will be referred to as such in this book.

Chaplaincy is not something new but has a long wonderful history in the United States. The first Chaplain in America came over on the Mayflower, and signed the Mayflower Compact long before the founding of our country. George Washington assigned Chaplains to the military during the Revolutionary war. Chaplains have a long wonderful history in the United States.

This book will discuss many general topics surrounding chaplaincy, but it is specifically designed for those working with first responders—more specifically, law enforcement. There is a very real need today to understand the demands upon the law enforcement family, and how to minister to their specific needs. These needs will be addressed from a practical, Chaplain perspective. I am a Christian, a follower of Jesus Christ, and I write from that stand point. There are Chaplains of other faiths that may have a different theology, but our philosophy of serving law enforcement will likely be much the same.

SECTION I

This section will examine the transformation a rookie cop goes through the transformation from being altruistic, and passionate about police work, to being critical and expecting only the worst from people. This is a subtle but remarkable change often taking place over an entire career.

SECTION II

This section discusses how this change often leads to compromise in an officer's character and integrity. Law enforcement is a career field with a disproportionably large percentage of divorce, alcoholism, stress related illnesses and injuries and even suicide.

SECTION III

Section three gives practical advice and instruction in areas of ministry to officers. It discusses how the Chaplain can come along-side the officer, and re-enforce his or her character. The Chaplain must earn the trust and respect of the officer. In doing this they will earn the privilege of speaking into his or her life.

SECTION IV

The last section briefly addresses how to establish a Chaplaincy program, and what a Chaplain can do hands on, in areas of prevention, postvention, and caring intervention. It offers answers to questions on how to intervene in officer's lives, to help keep them healthy, and prevent the kind of self-defeating and self-destructive thinking and behavior that so many officers fall victim to.

Thank you for picking up this book. I have known and been mentored by some wonderful, gifted Chaplains. My hope in writing this book is to pass on what I have learned

from them and experienced myself, and provide tools
useful in make you a better Chaplain-- if you already serve
in this capacity-- and help those who may be considering
the dynamic life-changing ministry that is Chaplaincy. My
prayer is that you will be one to "pick up the baton" and
carry it as we run this race together.

SECTION I
FOUNDATIONAL STRENGTHS CONFOUNDED

Chaplain Terry Morgan

CHAPTER 1
SO WHAT'S SO SPECIAL ABOUT BEING A COP

Romans 13:1-6 *"Obey the Government for God is the one who has put it there. There is no government anywhere that God has not placed in power. So those who refuse to obey the laws of the land are refusing to obey God, and punishment will follow. For the policeman does not frighten people who are doing right; but those doing evil will always fear him. So if you don't want to be afraid, keep the laws and you will get along well. The policeman is sent by God to help you. But if you are doing something wrong, of course you should be afraid, for he will have you punished. He is sent by God for that very purpose. Obey the laws, then for two reasons: first to keep from being punished, and second just because you know you should.*

Pay your taxes too, for these same two reasons. For government workers need to be paid so that they can keep on doing God's work, serving you."(1)

What is so special about being a cop? Lt. Col. Dave Grossman talks about different personality types in his book "On Killing". Grossman talks about a particular veteran he interviewed while doing research for this book. He suggested that people could be grouped together into three very basic categories. In his words, "One veteran I interviewed told me that he thought of most of the world as sheep: gentle, decent, kindly creatures who are essentially incapable of true aggression. In this veteran's mind there is another human subspecies (of which he is a member) that is a kind of dog: faithful, vigilant creatures who are very much capable of aggression when circumstances require. But, according to his model, there are wolves (sociopaths) and packs of wild dogs (gangs and aggressive armies) abroad in the land, and the sheepdogs (the soldiers and policemen of the world) are environmentally and biologically predisposed to be the ones who confront these predators." (2)

Lt. Col. Grossman goes on to say, "I have met these men, these "sheepdogs," over and over again as I interviewed veterans.".... "They would not misuse or misdirect their aggression any more than a sheepdog would turn on his flock, but in their hearts many of them yearn for a righteous battle, a wolf upon whom to legitimately and lawfully turn their skills." (3)

According to the comparison by Lt. Col. Grossman, the majority of people in society should be labeled as sheep. There is nothing wrong with being a sheep. Sheep are productive members of society, contributing to the well being of the community as a whole. Most sheep could get along very well with little interference-- eating grass and producing wool. But then the wolves creep in, and begin stalking, troubling, and even attacking the sheep. These wolves are the very small percentage of any culture that makes up the criminal element. Only between two to three percent of our society is considered career criminals, or wolves.

There is another small group of people that counterbalance these wolves. They are the sheep dogs; those in our society with the disposition to protect the sheep. Only 3%-- a very small number of people-- would be labeled as sheep dogs. Sheep dogs look out for the peace, security and safety of the sheep. These individuals are the core of those men and women who answer the call to become law enforcement officers, soldiers, and other first responders.

The "sheepdogs" or police officers are those uncommon and exceptional people who run toward the sound of gunfire. Instead of running away from danger, as most people would, they rush to try to rescue whoever is in trouble. They would never intentionally harm one of the sheep they have sworn to protect. They are, in fact, often known to lay their lives down to protect any one of these sheep without hesitation.

"Sheepdogs" are a rare and special breed, and make up a very small percentage of humanity; however, they are vital to our survival, and our security. If not for these brave officers-- these sheepdogs-- the sheep would be scattered and killed by the packs of ravenous wolves.

Lt. Col. Grossman's analogy can be taken one-step further. Grossman brilliantly described the relationships between the sheep and sheepdog, and the danger posed by the wolves and packs of wild dogs. I propose that there are other groups within our populace. These groups of people are the shepherds-- shepherds who look after the sheep. They are more commonly known as pastors, or priests. Each shepherd has his own "flock" of sheep that he has the responsibility of guiding, teaching and protecting. However, there are a select few belonging to a unique group who have the privilege of looking after the spiritual, mental, and emotional well being of the "sheepdog". This chaplain role is to be there for the well being of the police officer, just as the shepherd is there for the well being of the sheepdog.

The Bible talks about these special people in Romans 13 quoted earlier that say God calls the Police Officer and those who obey the law need have no fear of the Police officer. However, he that does not obey the law should definitely be afraid, because the police officer doesn't carry the sword (or a side arm) in vain. The Bible very clearly and specifically says that officers are called to this work. It is more than just a job, or a career to them, just as being a pastor, or minister is more than just a job. It is a calling from God. They are called by God to be police officers just as much and just as truly as some of us are called to be ministers.

God whispers in the ear of a young man or young woman calling them out by name to be different from their peers. They are called to a higher level of responsibility and faithful service. F.F. Bruce, a professor of Biblical Criticism and exegesis, and a Biblical Commentator, confirms this call to law enforcement as a call to ministry. Referring to the passage in Romans 13, he states "But it is plain that Paul envisages two quite distinct spheres of 'service' to God. 'The sanction that the Bible, here and elsewhere, gives to the forcible restraint of evil puzzles many modern Christians, because of its apparent contradiction to Christ's way of love and His precept of non-resistance to evil. But this comes from failing to distinguish the truth is that the Bible affirms both the Law "which worketh wrath (Rom. IV 15) and the "faith which worketh by love" (4)

Law enforcement officers are a very special segment of the population. Not everyone would want to be a police officer. Moreover, of those who do want to be a law enforcement officer, only a small percentage have all the right "ingredients" to do the work. As mentioned before, only about 3% of our population could qualify to become a law enforcement officer, due to the rigorous requirements. (5)

A considerable amount of work is required just to be considered for the law enforcement training academy. Not every person having a desire to become an officer can get through the intense screening process. A very small percentage actually makes it through this first phase.

A candidate must go through several steps before being accepted into the police academy. First there is a written test, which measures general aptitude based on the skills needed to be a police officer. They will gage such things as observation skills; decision-making; and map reading and directional orientation. Reading comprehension and written ability is checked to make sure the applicant can follow technical instructions, and write reports.

Next, there is a physical ability test. This is a very rigorous and physically demanding test to make sure a person can handle the physical requirements of police work. The test may entail such things as running a 500-yard obstacle course, climbing over three to six foot walls, and dragging a 150 pound "simulated victim" - while wearing a heavy bullet proof vest and racing against the clock.

A thorough background check will be performed ensuring no criminal history of any kind. Only the best of the best need apply for law enforcement. Employment and any military history will likely be investigated as well. A person's life is put under a microscope.

A polygraph test is often performed ensuring truthfulness on the background information as well as any other illegal practices that may not appear on the background examination. The examiners want to verify the honesty and integrity of the applicant. A person who is not honest in little things, can discredit anything they say in a court of law.

Viable candidates will likely have to meet with a professional psychologist for further screening. Applicants will have to be found free of any emotional or mental conditions which might have an adverse affect on the work of a law enforcement officer. Answers on earlier exams may again also be examined for truthfulness.

Finally, a medical examination will be conducted to make sure no health problems exist that could potentially limit the applicant's ability to perform police work duties. Vision is also important. A candidate will need to be able to see measurably well, even if they wear corrective lenses, or contacts.

Generally speaking, all of these tests are on a pass or fail basis. If a person fails a test, they may be eligible at a later time to try again; however, all of the tests must be passed before consideration for application to attend a police academy.

Training to become a law enforcement officer, after passing the "gauntlet" of tests to become accepted to the academy, is another challenge in and of itself. There are mental, physical, and emotional challenges as well being stretched to or beyond the limit. Among courses included are principles of law enforcement, criminal law, rules of evidence, search and seizure, laws of arrest and control methods, traffic laws, juvenile laws, first aid, care and use of firearms, patrol theory and methods, as well as physical conditioning, self-defense, and weapons training. The law enforcement academy course runs normally around 32 weeks. This includes 6 weeks of field training. At any time during the course of training at the academy the candidate may be failed clear up to the last day of class. Assignment to a department and further field training follows after satisfactory completion occurs.

An experienced officer, usually called a field-training officer, or FTO, will mentor the recruit. They will ride and work with an FTO (or several FTOs) usually for a period of several months. During that time, they will be observed, scrutinized, critiqued, and evaluated. At the end of field training, they will still be monitored, as they enter a time of probation lasting often a year.

At long last, if they make it through this entire ordeal, they will finally become a full-fledged law enforcement officer. (6)

Returning to the question that needs to be asked: What is so special about being a cop?

Analogies have been made comparing law enforcement officers to the ancient knightly order of the Paladin. Both wore armor. The knight wore a suit of mail, while the cop wears a bulletproof vest. The knight wore a sword at his side to help him keep the peace, while the cop wears a gun. The Paladin carried a shield with the crest of the kingdom he served, close to and protecting his heart, and as a symbol of his authority, while the officer wears a shield called a badge on his or her left side over their heart. This represents their agency and the authority they have been given to serve and to protect. The resemblance of an officer to a knight after the order of the Paladin is striking.

A closer look at the history of the Paladin shows today's law enforcement officer has a close resemblance to the noble knights of old. The order of Paladin actually began before the time of the knights, in the 8th century when Charlemagne put together a band of twelve powerful soldiers who commanded his troops. The soldier's assignment was to protect Charlemagne from bodily harm. He named this group, "The Twelve Paladins of Charlemagne". The most famous of these twelve was a knight named Roland written about in the ancient song, the "Song of Roland". The song paints a picture of bravery and loyalty. It tells the tale of how this Paladin, heroically gave his life holding back the enemy forces allowing Charlemagne more time to retaliate.

Around the middle of the 9th century, a group of French peasants were hired as warriors. They were given ornate and powerful armor to wear, and their skill with horsemanship quickly won the heart of their king. We are familiar with this as the beginning of the age of the knights decked in their shining armor and riding their noble steeds.

The social status of the knights was greatly elevated in the 11th century when the Church gave them its official sanction. The Church declared that the order of knighthood was a sacred office ordained by God (likely based on Romans 13), and made the appointment of new knights into a holy ritual. They swore their allegiance and loyalty to the king and the Church, much as our officer's today take an oath of office when they are sworn in.

Now sanctioned by the Church the knights were given a new set of responsibilities, based on the code of chivalry. The code of chivalry was a set of principles based on religious ideals. The knight now epitomized the highest standards of moral behavior and the peasants as well as the royalty they served under, had deep admiration for them.

The Chivalric Code was taken in the 11th century during the time of the crusades. The Paladin knights took an oath of honor to hold to chivalry. The Chivalric Code went something like this:

Thou shalt believe all that the church teaches and shall obey all her commandments.

Thou shalt defend the church.

Thou shalt respect all weaknesses and shalt constitute thyself the defender of them.

Thou shalt love the country in which thou wast born.

Thou shalt not recoil before thine enemy.

Thou shalt make war against the infidel without cessation and without mercy.

Thou shalt perform scrupulously thy feudal duties, if they be not contrary to the laws of God.

Thou shalt never lie, and shalt remain faithful to thy pledged word.

Thou shalt be generous, and give largesse to everyone.

Thou shalt be everywhere and always the champion of the Right and the Good against injustice and evil. (7)

The Paladins fought for duty to their king and their God, maintaining their devotion without coercion, or expectation of reward. They idealized righteousness in their behavior. (8) Law enforcement officers serve in much the same way out of a sense of duty, and moral courage.

"So what's so special about being a cop?" The answer to this question is not easily answered. We have addressed various aspects of what makes a law enforcement officer special. The call... The testing... The training... The commitment...all are integral parts.

Our law enforcement officers are asked to do a job that most of us would not want to do. They are asked to lay their lives on the line to protect us. They are asked to go into dangerous places, to deal with dangerous people, and be a peacemaker; they are asked to sacrifice time with their family, miss holidays, and special events, all to keep the average citizen safe; and to do all of these things with very little if any thanks. They are asked to do things that aren't fair to ask from anyone, and to do them without complaining

If you asked a room full of law enforcement cadets why they chose to become cops, there would be little surprise in their response. Most every one of them would answer similarly, "I want to do something to make a difference."

The process of elimination that officers must go through, and why they should be considered a very special group of people is evident. It would be easy to put them on a pedestal as something more than human as efficient emotionless robots. We could rely on them to be perfectly oiled machines, maintaining our security so we can sleep peacefully at night. As unfeeling automatons they would always be there when we needed them, and would not be affected by the horrible awful sights and sounds they experienced every day. But the reality is they are no more robots than you or me.

As Clarence M. Kelly, a former Director of the Federal Bureau of Investigation says, "The time has come for Americans to understand and appreciate – the humanitarian nature of the Law Enforcement profession – in more than thirty years in the Law Enforcement profession, I have known thousands of officers – they are human. They have emotions." (9)

In the following pages, and chapters, you will see a gradual transformation. It is not a pretty change. It is a change that we would and should prevent if possible. You will see how the law enforcement officer venture out altruistic and ready to "save the world", and yet end up being cold, hard, and cynical.

(handwritten annotation: "Intervention System" enclosed in parentheses with asterisks on both sides)

CHAPTER 2
THE WELL WORN PATH FROM ALTRUISM TO CYNICISM

The evidence is overwhelming. Countless law enforcement officers go through a transformation. They are changed by their experiences as a cop. This is not a change for the better for most of them, but a degradation of their character, which can lead to acute mental, emotional, spiritual and even physical problems.

Many young officers, in the early part of their career may fancy themselves as a "John (or Jane) Wayne" type character. They see themselves wearing the white hat, cruising in with their noble steed (their patrol car) to take care of the bad guys and save the day. Their families see them as heroes, and admire and look up to them. After a few years, their attitudes seem to change. They begin portraying more of a "Dirty Harry (or Dirty Harriet)" image. They see only the negative in every situation and expect the worst from everyone they meet. They develop an attitude that "Everyone is guilty of something".

The inexperienced officer, fresh out of academy, generally has an altruistic mind set. They are ready to go out and save the world. Webster's Dictionary defines Altruism as a "Selfless regard for the well being of others." (10) You could use the analogy that the altruism the officer feels as they first begin their career in law enforcement is like a granite block. This block is large and solid, seemingly unbreakable. It embodies their moral character, their work ethic, and their values. It is the officer's foundation upon which their lives, and careers are built.

When the officer begins field training, he or she begins to see that the work is somewhat different from what they expected. Of course they were told what would happen in their academy, but they thought it would be different for them. They have to work odd hours, with complicated day off schedules. Their "weekend" may fall in the middle of the week now. Frequently, they have to work on holidays and miss family events. "It's alright though," they think. "I'm tough and can handle it". Meanwhile, there is a small, almost invisible little crack that forms in their solid granite block of altruism.

The peace officer's job tends to be a series of highs and lows. The officer goes from call, to call, to call. They may go from a crime in progress, --flying through intersections with their lights and sirens flashing -- to confronting two rival gangs -- then to a high speed pursuit. Their next call may be to investigate an abandoned stolen vehicle in a field. They may have to sit and wait for what seems like hours for a tow truck as it slowly meanders -- like a cow coming home to the barn at milking time -- to haul off the vehicle. There are many highs and lows in the adrenaline level as an officer goes from the excitement of pursuing and capturing a criminal to the slow mundane police work. This often causes a temporary depression. Their adrenaline is pumped up, and then wears off -- repeatedly throughout the day. Still, they can handle it. "They're tough, and this is what they signed on to do." Another small crack forms in another area of their seemingly invulnerable foundation.

Then there are the calls that absolutely change a person forever. The first time an officer arrives on a really bad scene, involving homicides, suicides, fatal car crashes, and especially deaths of a child or infant, he or she may never be the same. It is as if something gets on them and regardless of how much scrubbing is done, it can't be washed off.   On one occasion an officer rushed to the scene where an infant had stopped breathing. It was an apparent SIDS (sudden Infant Death Syndrome) where an infant had stopped breathing. The officer was the first on the scene, beating the paramedics by two or three minutes. The frantic parents thrust their still child into the hands of the officer and begged, "Please, do something!" The officer began CPR while thinking of her own baby lying in bed at home. The child in her arms was stiff and cold. The life had long since left her but still the officer tries to breathe life into its frail little body. She knew it was too late. The baby was already gone. But the officer could not bear the thought of looking into the pleading eyes of the parents and telling them there was nothing more she could do.

Perhaps it is the call where a child has endured months of physical abuse, as evidenced by the old bruises, cigarette burns, and half healed scars all over his body. A drugged up father finally beat the poor thing to death. On calls such as this, officers see the very worst of society. They are instantly changed and will not be the same again. Sometimes they know there was a change, and they "hear" the crack form in that granite block.

After seeing a horrible scene, most officers are expected to go on to their next call, and continue to be professional. They return to their patrol car shaken then realize they have "three more calls pending" waiting for them to respond. They may go from a horrible graphic scene to a domestic disturbance. They may see a husband and wife "at each other's throats" over something trivial while their child hides in the shadows. The officer may want to grab them both, shake them, and yell at them. "That child cowering in the hallway is what you should be concerned about not with who caused the check book to be out of balance." But the officers are trained to be professional. They handle the call, just like the previous ten this week while they ache inside. Over the years the officer will see many graphic horrible scenes. The solid granite block that seemed to be so strong and stalwart a few years ago when they began this journey of service, now has cracks running all through it.

Over the course of a career, a law enforcement officer has to endure criticism from the department, as well as from those they have vowed to serve and protect. They face the challenges of balancing being a police officer with being a parent, a spouse or a son or daughter. They will put their lives on the line every day and are subject to an accumulation of stress that would cripple an ordinary person. All the while, they cram their emotions, and don't allow those around them to ever see their softer side, or show they are still human. They protect the ones they love the most, by not talking about the horrible things they have experienced – and their granite block of Altruism, now cracked and chipped, begins to crumble.

Officers see life extremes every day. Their philosophy begins shifting from "All people are basically good and only a few are bad" to "None can be trusted because all are bad people and no good ones are left". People constantly lie to them. Police officers deal with the four percent who make up the career criminal element on a regular basis so all they see is the bad. They are "shielded" from seeing the good in people.

A question was asked at a seminar, directed towards law enforcement officers: "What is the first thing you think of when you hear the phrase, 'Cub Scout Leader'?" The lecturer said that in an average crowd of people, most of the answers would be something along the lines of, "community leader", or "good dad". Among this group of law enforcement officers almost every hand went up when the question asked was, "How many thought of the word "pedophile". This demonstrates how the thinking of these officers had changed because of the horrible scenes they see every day.

A person who works with their hands can take pride in a job well done. A carpenter or brick mason can look at a building for years to come. Long after they retire they may see that building and have a warm feeling inside as they tell their grandkids, "I built that." They see houses or buildings as reference points. A police officer on the other hand may arrest a suspect in the morning and by evening

16

they are out on bail or released on a technicality. They see a stretch of road and it reminds them that the dark spot on the pavement marks the fatal crash site where a drunk driver killed that entire family. They look at a house and think about a drug dealer who was arrested and is now out on bail. This leads to a feeling of a lack of accomplishment.

Over time paranoia sets in and officers begins taking on an "Us vs. Them" mentality. They begin to associate and socialize only with other officers. They begin to be on a heightened state of alert all of the time. Ever noticed where police officers sit in a restaurant? They always sit in the back of a restaurant with their backs to the wall, where they can see what is going on around them and they can instantly react when something "goes down". An officer may begin showing symptoms of anger, alcohol/drug problems, domestic violence and even suicidal tendencies.

Altruism in a law enforcement officer is slowly transformed over time. It becomes something else -- much weaker, unstable and dangerous. The officer is constantly faced with the extremes of life. They must respond to suicides, dead babies, fatal car crashes, sexual assaults, homicides, and people attacking other people. When altruism is destroyed, it is transformed into something called cynicism. Cynicism affects every area of the person's life. When an officer becomes cynical, they compromise their own values and character. They become insecure and aggressive and all areas of the officer's life begins to suffer. (11) The Webster's dictionary definition of cynic is, "One who believes all human action has selfish motives." (12)

Many factors contribute to this change with the number one cause being stress. This can come in many different forms. When we think of stress, we usually think of it in negative terms. However, it can be positive depending on a person's reaction.

Stress is a part of every day in some way or another with the most common simply called "normal stress". Normal stress causes wear and tear on a person's body but normal coping skills effectively nullify it. This can also be defined simply as "life".

The good things that happen to us in life are called "eu-stress". Examples of eu-stress are a new job, buying your first home, a baby, getting married, etc. These are significant gains in our lives but can also be the source of stress.

When we think of stress, we usually think more often of "distress". Distress describes those times we experience significant losses. These experiences would be the opposite of eu-stress and would include such things as getting fired from a job, losing a home, getting divorced, etc. These types of situations take a lot higher toll on our coping skills and are much more difficult to handle.

Stress built up over time is called cumulative stress. This can come from not dealing well with the little every day stressors. It can also come from adding distress to an already significant build up of normal stress. (A stressor is the stimulus that causes, rouses up, draws forth or is related to the stress response.) This is generally the kind of stress that leads to burnout. Burnout is a state of being mentally and physically exhausted.

The last kind of stress is what is known as critical incident stress. Critical incident stress is relatively rare although almost everyone must face it at one time or another. Critical incidents are such things as suddenly losing a loved one to death or being in genuine fear of your life. Calibre Press, Inc. gives the definition of a critical incident as "Any situation that forces you to face your own vulnerability and mortality, or potentially overwhelms your ability to cope. A critical incident is characterized by being sudden and unexpected, and disrupts your sense of control, and beliefs in how the world works." (13) Jeffrey T. Mitchell, Ph.D. developed what has come to be known as the "Dr. Jeffrey Mitchell Model of Critical Incident Stress Management". He defines a critical incident as it directly affects a law enforcement officer as "any incident that causes emergency service personnel to experience unusually strong emotional reactions which have the potential to interfere with their ability to function either at the scene or later". (14)

In the previous chapter, we established that police officer's are specially gifted and unique people. They have a vital and fairly uncommon position in society. With that uniqueness it can be presumed they experience unique kinds of stressors.

Almost any single stressor in law enforcement can be found in other careers. For example, EMTs often respond to the same shootings as law enforcement officers and see the same terrible graphic scenes. Reporters and photographers often are exposed to graphic scenes either in person or while editing footage for news broadcasts. The unique aspect of law enforcement from other occupations is all the different stressors appear in one job. As Glenn Norstrem, a 26 year veteran of the St. Paul Police Department once said, "There is no getting away from stress as a police officer. Stress is part of the job." (15) Many officers suffer from chronic stress.

The constant stress of a position in law enforcement can have a number of damaging physical, emotional and even spiritual effects on an officer. When an officer is affected by stress, it takes its toll on their job performance, family life and the law enforcement agency where they work.

A whole list of things can be attributed to stress. "Commonly reported effects of stress for law enforcement officers include the following: cynicism and suspiciousness, emotional detachment, post-traumatic stress disorder, heart attacks, ulcers, weight gain, and other health problems, suicide, reduced efficiency in performing duties, reduced morale, excessive aggressiveness and an increase in citizen complaints, alcoholism and other substance abuse, marital or other relationship and family problems (e.g., extramarital affairs, divorce, or domestic violence)." (16) Stress affects the behavior of the officer, and contributes to absenteeism and early retirement.

Stress, over time, will manifest itself in a law enforcement officer's life in a fairly predictable pattern. At first stress will likely be an underlying force. Have you ever watched a flooded river carrying whole tress and other large debris? Often a tree will float down a swollen river just below the surface of the water. These trees are called "killer snags." Stress, like that tree, may be below the surface, but equally dangerous. Over time the stress will become apparent. It will "break surface" in such ways as excessive drinking/drugs and/or an unacceptably high number of citizen complaints. The stress will eventually become debilitating. The tree going along below the surface of the water will suddenly explode up full of power with a life of its own wiping out anything in its path. The final result of too much stress is a poor and inadequate job performance, severe health problems, alcoholism or drug abuse, and very possibly an officer "eating their own gun" (suicide).

Many stressors ultimately take a toll on the police office's family. An officer going down the path towards cynicism tends to communicate less and less with their spouse and children. They begin using dark, or gallows humor, as a defense mechanism to avoid dealing with problems at home. They have to handle everyone's problems all day and problems at home seem trivial by comparison. As the officer gets more established in the police subculture (the blue wall) they begin to isolate themselves more and more from the "outside world". However, the officer's family has to live in that outside world.

Shift work compounds the tension on the officer and his or her family. Shift work changes weekly and oftentimes they are working when their spouse is home and home when their spouse is working. Holidays off are rare (criminals never take a holiday), and the weekend is often in the middle of the week. This tends to make the spouse feel isolated. The world around them goes on while the officer often is unable to attend various functions because of their work schedule. Invitations must often be declined, holidays are postponed, and recreation may become solo activities for the spouse and the officer.

Emotional Isolation is even worse than the physical isolation caused by shift work and the mental isolation caused by the police mentality. A romantic rendezvous doesn't happen as often. The officer and spouse sleep alone as they are on different shifts. The stress of being in law enforcement and dealing with trauma, danger and violence every day causes them to cram their emotions. They do this to keep up a professional demeanor at all times. Emotions are hard to turn back on after they have been turned off and suppressed for so long.

Pressure on an officer can be made worse if relationships at home are strained. The typical cop holds their family up as very important. When things are not going right at home, it can throw off their whole sense of balance. On the other hand, an officer's family can be a source of great support and stability and one of the biggest relievers of stress. This subject is discussed further in section III.

The effect of stress on the officer, magnified by pressures at home, will be manifested at the station house and agency. The most obvious manifestation on the job is the impaired performance and reduction in productivity. The officer's morale and self esteem is slashed. As dominos falling, this leads to more public relations problems through such things as accusations of police brutality and political in-fighting within the department as well as absenteeism and tardiness. Some officers will eventually take an early retirement as a consequence of stress related problems.

Cynicism will weaken an officer's moral character. They may give in to temptation and do things they would not even consider under ordinary circumstances. They may commit crimes themselves. When an officer has a moral failure, the media eats it up. The media will expose the entire department to open censure and criticism. Any time the "righteous fall", it is front page news. This is very similar to a well-known minister falling into sin and getting caught. Both the officer and the minister are held to a higher standard and make a much bigger "story" when they fall. This type of negative publicity causes a diminished public trust for an entire agency-- not just the officer involved.

CHAPTER 3
FIVE MAJOR STRESSES
OF LAW ENFORCEMENT

Different people react differently to highly stressful situations. Some people seem to have a natural ability to remain calm during the most challenging times. Others may have an adrenaline spike then quickly recover. Still others will react negatively to traumatic events and maintain a heightened stress level long after others have leveled off.

The reaction of law enforcement to stressors will be dependent upon a variety of issues including their personality, their background, training, experience, years on the job, and a variety of other influences. Most professionals involved in counseling law enforcement officers agree there are four or five certain general classes that most stressors fall into. "Sources of stress that seem to be common among—and in some cases unique or particularly burdensome to – law enforcement officers fall into four categories: (1) those related to the law enforcement organization, (2) those that relate to law enforcement work, (3) those that stem from the actions of the criminal justice system and the general public, and (4) those related to the individual officer's personal life and approach to stressful events." (17)

Stressors in law enforcement come from a variety of sources. Working with the general public can not only be stressful, but sometimes life threatening. The department itself has its own challenges as an officer tries to do the job they were hired for. The job may involve seeing things such as suicides, death of children, and may even involve taking a human life. These interactions and others are common place with the average officer.

Cops have a very special bond with each other. The confidence they share with each other is very similar to what soldiers experience in battle. They develop a trust and camaraderie as they depend on their partners and watch each other's back. Their partners, fellow officers from their Watch, and members of their department become like extended family. There is an adhesiveness that forms between them. They tend to only let other officers into their circle of influence, and bare their souls to one another. This is sometimes referred to as the thin blue wall. This is at least in part why it is so stressful for an officer to have trouble from those in authority over them. They are fellow cops.

Administrative support, and rewards or recognition for good work are both very important to an officer. Badges and ribbons are symbols of honor, courage, hard work, and dedication. A simple pat on the back from a cop's commanding officer during a briefing before a shift can go a long way towards limiting stress and promoting healthy thinking. After a good word is publicly spoken about an officer for a job well done, especially in front of his or her peers, other officers will think, "Wow, I want to do a good job, so maybe next time it will be me getting praise from the sergeant."

On the other hand, the hurt and disappointment felt by officers who feel they have been wronged by their commanding officers can be devastating. A harsh word spoken to an officer from someone of higher rank, especially after a critical incident, can cut through them emotionally like a knife.

An officer in management will receive a lot more respect from those under their command if they take the time to show they care about their troops. A great example is the captain or lieutenant who checks on their men and women after a dangerous encounter such as a shooting, or other critical incident. Major kudos goes to the commanding officer who checks in with each team member asking them if they are O.K. after a swat incident. Those in command should not just assume they are fine. Simply asking how they are doing will show that management cares about them, and will go a long way in promoting loyalty to the department.

I recall responding to a SWAT call late one night. A wanted dangerous fugitive had been reported being at a house with a history of drugs. The SWAT team coordinated their strategy to get him out with minimum resistance. They showed up in force around 2 a.m. They surrounded the house and began moving in. One of the people in the house decided to go out on the porch to smoke a cigarette. He flipped a switch as he walked out the door, and suddenly several of the team members were backlit by a lamp post at the end of the driveway. Before the cops could put out the light, the person on the porch could be heard yelling, "Hey, there's somebody out there."

The situation quickly changed from being a fairly routine surprise raid, to a hostage situation. They had lost the element of surprise. The suspect had a number of fire arms inside and immediately started shooting. The SWAT team members could not get a clear shot without the risk of hitting one of the hostages. To make a long story short, after firing off over a hundred rounds, the suspect stuck his hand out the door to fire his 45, and one of the SWAT team managed to shoot him in the hand. The suspect immediately surrendered after that. None of the SWAT team were injured in this event. It could have ended much differently.

I walked into the crime scene with the lieutenant to the command post. I observed him as he stopped by each SWAT officer he came across. He asked if they were O.K., and shook their hands, and spoke a few words of encouragement to each of them. This spoke volumes to the SWAT team. They knew the Lieutenant cared what happened to them. Another commander was criticized for walking past them without saying a word or even acknowledging them.

As has previously been noted, the most common sources of stress for a law enforcement officer come as the direct result of the agencies they work for. The policies and procedures of their agencies can cause a substantial amount of stress in an officer's life. Note that the Chaplain should never be tempted to take sides in issues involving an officer and their command staff or the department. The Chaplain is the Chaplain to all of the officers, both the line and command staff, and cannot afford to become entangled in office politics or to be anything but neutral. Picking sides may seem to draw some cops closer at first; but in the end it will drive a wedge between the Chaplain and the whole department.

The Chaplain needs to be careful to never give the impression that they are "in the pocket", or notifying management about line officers. When you make an office visit, start with the highest ranking officer first. In other words, go see the chief first instead of last after you have talked with the line officers. There is a very important reason for this. Going to see a commander after visiting with line officers may give the appearance that you are reporting on your conversations with them. Don't underestimate appearances or how suspicious cops tend to be.

Another major source of stress from the department is shift work. Shift work refers to regular non-overtime employment outside of the 7:00 A.M. to 6:00 P.M. work schedule. The origin of shift work can be traced back to around 1860. It was not begun with police officers or even firemen but bakers. By around 1927, studies were begun to measure the effects of shift work on the human body.

The human body has an internal, biological clock, also known as the "circadian rhythm". This clock controls many bodily functions. Over the course of the day and night there are highs and lows in body temperature, urine production and blood steroids. Studies of the human body have discovered that the human body cannot adjust instantaneously to changes in routine such as a work schedule. So in effect, getting enough sleep becomes a major issue for a person working shift work, and especially a rotating shift.

Most officers, especially those that do shift work, develop what is called a "sleep debt". There have been studies in sleep deprivation, that show those who work shift work get less sleep per 24 hour period than those that don't work shift work. On average, the person doing shift work gets seven hours less sleep per week than those working regular day shifts. Those people who work a night or rotating shift averaged only five and a half hours of sleep per 24 hour period. This sleep deprivation will lead to slowed reaction time, exhaustion, and stress. In fact, the cumulative effect of sleep deprivation on the law enforcement officer has been shown to aggravate job stress, and the ability of the officer to deal with stress. (18)

Lt. Colonel Dave Grossman talks about the problem of sleep deprivation in his seminar "On Killing". He specifically talks about a soldier doing demanding strenuous work for multiple days without a break. He then breaks down the hours of sleep this person gets per day, and how their efficiency goes down with the number of hours they sleep. Here is how he broke it down:

"After 20 days of demanding, continuous physical activity:
    -7 hours of sleep per day = 87% of peak efficiency
    -6 hours of sleep per day = 50% of peak efficiency
    -5 hours of sleep per day = 28% of peak efficiency
    -4 hours of sleep per day = 15% of peak efficiency
Lack of Sleep = key factor in stress casualties and PTSD" (19) The implications are pretty clear when you consider that many officers put in an excessive amount of overtime on top of working shift work. Working more and longer hours results in less time for rest, sleep, and rejuvenation.

Other sources of stress from the law enforcement agency may include such things as negative management styles, inconsistent discipline and enforcement of rules, equipment deficiencies and shortages, and real or perceived favoritism regarding assignments, and promotions.

There are some officers who may have additional reasons to find their law enforcement agency a source of stress. Women and other minorities in law enforcement may face a variety of additional stressors. They may face harassment, and even job discrimination. They may feel they have to be better than their fellow officers. They may push themselves to prove to themselves and others that they belong in law enforcement.

Minority officers face challenges that most officers don't have to consider. "Some female, gay, and minority officers may have the added stress of a lack of acceptance by the predominantly white, male force and subsequent denial of needed information, alliances, protection, and sponsorship from supervisors and colleagues; lack of role models and mentors; pressure to prove oneself to colleagues and the public; exclusion from informal channels of support; and lack of influence on decision-making." (20) These groups each have some common, and some unique issues. There are particular challenges for each of these groupings.

One of the causes of stress among minority officers comes simply because of their lack of numbers in most departments. "Despite the increasing presence of women in law enforcement, the profession remains very male-dominated and "macho", resulting in the prevalence of certain attitudes, values and expectation, including traditional ideas regarding appropriate gender roles and behaviors." (21)

The issue of gay and lesbian police officers in particular is a very thorny issue, which truly needs to be formally addressed. Chaplains working with law enforcement do not have the luxury of being in a church congregation, where most everyone attending does so because they have similar beliefs. As a Chaplain you are expected to be "The Chaplain" for all faiths, and beliefs. People, especially officers, will be watching us, and we need to be informed and know how to behave, react to, and treat all of them.

28

We cannot afford to show favoritism, or respect to one and not another.

This book is in no way meant to be an exhaustive theological exegetical treatise on the Biblical view on homosexuality, or transgender issues. As a Chaplain, it is vital that we stay non-political and non-judgmental towards all of our officers. If we are asked for our opinion as a Chaplain on **any** political issue, not just our view on homosexuality or transgender, it is vital that we give no public opinion. We are of no use to officers that we offend because of our outspoken views on such issues, no matter how good our intentions are. This is especially true in this age of instant "live" media coverage. A statement made regarding homosexuality that is caught on the news would immediately polarize us from either one camp or another (those either pro or opposed to the practice of homosexuality). The Chaplain would quite possibly lose not only their credibility but their position with a law enforcement organization.

The book of James talks a lot about showing favoritism. It specifically deals with the Church showing favoritism to the rich, simply because they have money, and thereby influence. This teaching can effectively be applied to the Chaplain working with law enforcement officers. They may not be wealthy but they may have other reasons for us to treat them favorably or not so favorably. We absolutely should not show favoritism to one officer simply because he or she is gay or straight. James 1:10 tells us "For whoever keeps the whole law and yet stumbles at just one point is guilty of breaking all of it." (22) We are sworn, as Chaplains, to work with all officers regardless of who they are; their lifestyle, their political views, or even their favorite sports team. From this passage of scripture in James, and other scripture verses, the case can easily be made that all sin is the same in God's eyes. There are not degrees, or levels of sin. There may be different consequences to our sins, even as there are different consequences to our actions. As a Christian, I believe that sin is sin, and there is no whitewashing it. However, the sin in homosexuality lies in the sexual act outside of marriage. In that light, a heterosexual couple having sex outside of marriage is just as guilty of sin as a homosexual couple engaging in sex. If we as Chaplains try to make one sin worse than another, e.g. saying homosexuality is worse than being heterosexual in a sexual relationship outside of marriage, are we not practicing "favoritism" as James directs us not to?

The bottom line for the Chaplain, whether you agree theologically with me or not, is simply this. It is better to be completely resigned to having no public opinion on homosexuality, or any other political issue. Besides all that, our concern should not be in making our opinion known, but to minister, and be the Chaplain to all of our officers. Law Enforcement officers are suffering enough stress in their career. There is already an added stress of being openly gay or lesbian in a primarily "macho" male dominated line of work. They don't need the Chaplain preaching to them or condemning them about their lifestyle. Leave that in God's hands to deal with as He sees fit. He is a lot wiser than any of us.

There are some very specific, unique issues in working with gay or lesbian officers. Knowing these issues will help us effectively minister to them.

The gay or lesbian officer may face discrimination if they let others know of their sexual orientation. The mutual acceptance and support of their fellow officers is essential in staying safe and effective as a cop. If the officer has not "come out of the closet", they may feel extra pressure because they don't feel like they are being totally honest and open. They may weigh the risks and consequences of being open about their sexual orientation, or keeping it secret.

By the way, if an officer confides in you that they are homosexual, it is vital to your ministry that you keep their secret. It is up to them if they choose to disclose this. You have a moral and ethical obligation (if not a legal one) to keep this information confidential.

Discrimination and harassment may be the biggest obstacle to the gay or lesbian officer. There may be real or perceived discrimination in getting a promotion, or getting a prime beat, or watch. This may add to their stress, and cause them to retire early, or have other stress related problems.

Women in law enforcement face similar struggles. Many women officers face the "good old boy" mentality. Many male officers tend not to accept women officers, and don't always take them seriously. They are often the target of sexual harassment.

There are a relatively few women who pursue law enforcement as a career. Many who do step up to the challenge retire early. According to a study done by the International Association of Chiefs of Police, some 57% of women who resign from law enforcement work, do so after an average of only two to five years. It should also be noted that the majority that did resign, approximately 73% were at the patrol officer rank. This may show they have a harder time getting promoted than their male counterparts. (23)

I have known personally at least a couple of women who have made it to the level of Chief of Police. They have struggled to overcome the stigmas, and have had to prove themselves over and over. But they made it and proved that it can be done. One in particular was from a very "traditional" city, with a great many people who opposed her. At the writing of this book, she is still there, and still doing a great job.

Our country has come a long way in racial relations. Still racial minorities face discrimination in many departments. They may feel left out, and unwelcome in some law enforcement circles. They may experience verbal abuse from other officers, supervisors, and even the public. The public may mistrust them because they are non-white (especially in predominantly Caucasian regions), and doubt their abilities to help resolve their problems. There may be real or perceived prejudice and discrimination in promotions, shifts, and beats.

Unfortunately, there may also be reverse discrimination taking place. Some (primarily white, male) officers perceive unfairness in affirmative action. This coupled with the heavy emphasis on always being politically correct, which has found its way into most departments, causes some to find an excuse to be prejudice against other races and ethnic groups.

While talking about various minority groups in law enforcement, it would be unfair to not mention one other group that is very commonly overlooked. The law enforcement support personnel are often forgotten when there is a crisis in the agency. For brevity, we could lump together support personnel to include dispatchers, community service officers, public information officers, secretarial staff, and other civilian employees. These people often have many of the same stressors as their law enforcement officer counterparts with the added problem of being seen as second-class employees. I have heard some cops referring to the difference between them and other law enforcement employees saying "Not sworn, not born."

Dispatchers who handle a traumatic incident call may need critical incident debriefing as much as the officers directly involved. They typically feel tremendously responsible for protecting "their officers" and may experience enormous guilt when things don't go right. If this is not addressed, the stress from this guilt can eat at the dispatcher, and become much worse over time. Dispatchers hear what is going on at a scene, but are relatively powerless to directly affect the outcome. In addition, they are often the last to know when everything is settled. The Chaplain needs to step up and make sure they are kept in the loop as soon as possible.

Most police agencies are run as a para-military organization, with a very distinct chain of command. "A police department is both a professional and military organization and these two aspects oppose each other." (24) Historically, the professional occupations were doctors, lawyers, ministers, and teachers. These professions require basic education, a bachelor's degree, and often more intense and specialized training and higher education. The professional then is licensed by an agency such as a medical board, an ordaining organization, etc. The professional person is then considered an expert in his or her field. They have a lot of discretion as to how they practice their profession, as they are expected to use their expertise in making good decisions.

Military tend to be the opposite of the professional occupations. Those in the military are very well trained; however they make very few decisions on their own. They are conditioned and trained to obey the chain of command without question. There are rules and regulations that cover virtually every area of a soldier's life.

Law enforcement officers are not professionals in the classic meaning of the word, though they are similar. Of course they must have a certain amount of education and training before they are selected. They usually must go through a law enforcement training academy. They are eventually sworn in and given authority by their department. They are expected to make good decisions based on their training, education and experience. However, just as a good soldier in the military, he or she has rules and procedures that must be followed.

The stress comes when the officer is forced to make a decision in the field. If he or she is able to make a good decision based on the rules and procedures they must follow, it's easy. However, how often does a call really go by the book? Often, the best solution to a problem will not be completely according to procedures. If the officer follows the rules set out for him or her, they will be in line with the department, but it may not satisfy the needs of the parties involved. If the officer goes outside of the procedures set by the department, the parties involved may be more satisfied with the outcome, but he or she risks being at odds with their department. If everything goes well, there is no fear of repercussions. But if things go poorly, the officer may have to answer for their decision and actions and for going against department policy.

One particular example where the administration can cross over into the area of stress from law enforcement work is in traffic stops. Cops do traffic stops every day for a variety of reasons. When officers make a stop they will hear almost any excuse from the passenger of the vehicle they have pulled over. Most of the time, they have come to expect the public to lie to them. They may be told anything from justifications or apologies meant to gain their sympathy to personal verbal attacks and indignities meant to demean and humiliate the officer.

There is always a chance that a routine traffic stop will quickly escalate into something far worse. Every traffic stop has the potential of turning into a life and death situation. Every officer making a traffic stop has to have the thought that this may be the person who attacks and try's to kill them. This is reality for them, and is a safety issue.

Part of the stress of doing a traffic stop is balancing safety, with courtesy. "If an officer approaches a car with a friendly attitude, his guard is down. He can't keep his defenses up and view a person as his friend at the same time. People are on guard against those they view as enemies, not friends. If an officer continually approaches cars with a friendly attitude, the chief will eventually get a call that one of his officers is lying in a pool of blood on the street." (25) Of course, if an officer approaches every traffic stop with a guarded attitude, their department will likely start getting complaints about them being cynical, and rude.

Looking at a person as either a friend or an enemy causes different mental states in a person. An officer can't hold both attitudes regarding a person at the same time. This is known in psychology as a double bind situation. Double bind situations are a huge source of psychological stress for anyone forced to experience them.

The next major source of stress for officers has to do with the kind of work they do, and the graphic scenes they see on the job. We all as taxpayers pay law enforcement officers to handle the parts of reality that we can't or don't want to ever have to deal with. They are paid to deal with the coarse, hard, mean streets, and the atrocities and carnage that go with them. We give them a badge and a gun, and ask them to deal with a world that is full of viciousness - the deranged, the sociopaths, the drunkards, and drug addicts are all part of their violent world. We ask them to handle all of the bloody, raw images of death in its many forms; from homicides, to suicides: from the natural, to the unnatural, and accidental. All of the very worst that life has to offer is laid on their plate.

The sights and sounds that most officers experience on a regular basis would astound, if not shock most people. Sergeant Steve Albrecht is a reserve officer with the San Diego Police Department, and is the author of the book "Fear & Violence on the Job: Prevention Solutions for the Dangerous Workplace". Here is what he has to say regarding these kinds of calls, "What might horrify the average civilian with no experience or knowledge of a city's traumatic events, i.e., the presence of a dead body in their neighborhood, a neighbor injured in a car accident, or a robbery that happened at their local branch or favorite convenience store, does not usually invoke a traumatic response in the average police officer." (26)

There once was a man with a sword walking through my neighborhood. He wore a ski mask over his face, and was making threatening gestures, and yelling obscenities. A person called 9-11 saying he was pounding on their door. When they looked out the peephole, he put the sword up to his mouth and licked the blade. When the person didn't answer the door, he walked down to the next house and did the same routine again.

The police responded and caught him trying to kick in a door. When the perpetrator saw them, he rushed at them with the sword. They shot him. He didn't die from the wounds, but it certainly stopped him.

The interesting thing was this call was just a minor story in the news. If I hadn't been called as a Chaplain I wouldn't have known anything about it. I mentioned this happened in my neighborhood. What I didn't mention was that my junior high aged daughter had stayed home sick from school that day. She had been home alone.

As a rookie officer the reality of being a protector of the public begins to quickly set in. The rookie cop may have high expectations of the job, thinking it will always be exciting, and rewarding, and suddenly have to face the long periods of boredom, and disrespect from the public they have sworn to protect. They may be justifiably worried about their competency and ability to do the job and the fear of doing something against regulations. They are closely monitored during probation. Many of the discomforts and stressors from being a rookie cop will pass with time, however, there are other stressors waiting to take their place.

There will be times when an officer calls for resources such as ambulances, or paramedics when they are not immediately available, especially in rural areas. The officer may be forced to try to keep victims calm while waiting for emergency medical personnel or others. They will often be the first on scene and may have to apply basic first aid and life saving techniques. This should be a footnote for Chaplains; what seems like a few minutes to a Chaplain responding to a scene at the request of an officer, may seem like an eternity to the cop trying to deal with emotional victims. When the Chaplain gets a call for an emergency response, they absolutely need to drop everything and get to the scene as quickly as possible without breaking any laws.

When you ask most officers about the very worst calls that they go on, the majority say it would be those involving children. Sergeant Albrecht goes on in his article on counter transference to talk about some of the symptoms and the horrible scenes that bring on counter transference. On this subject he says, "Other events that can take us out of our training and experience created comfort zones include the brutal rape of a young child, the murder of a person who reminds us of a family member or close friend, a multi-car accident involving people we know,

36

or a mass murder event, or any multiple victim homicide scene.

In these cases, the sheer size and immense pain of these traumas can cause us to doubt our once rock solid belief systems that we can cope with anything, anytime, anyplace." (27)

There are several interpretations of the word transference, or counter transference. For our purposes, a good working definition of transference is "When the wounds of the helper are triggered by the victims they are trying to help, by similarities between the victim and the helper, or by recent traumas in the life of the helper." (28) An example of this may be when an officer goes to an elder abuse call. In seeing the victim, the officer is reminded of his or her own grandfather, who died recently. Immediately, there is an emotional connection and impact. The officer may feel rage, or horror at the sight of "their grandpa" who has just been abused. Other symptoms of counter transference are dread, revulsion, shame, grief and/or mourning, and an overwhelming desire to get involved and directly intercede on the victim's behalf.

Let me give you an example of how transference can affect you. I responded to a multiple homicide/suicide. A man, estranged from his wife, shot his wife, her male friend, and all of his family members, then shot and killed himself. I was called to go to the hospital. One of the victims, a young boy, was unconscious but still alive. He had been shot in the head. I was assigned to the emergency room where doctors were futilely trying to save the young boy's life, while an officer stood by in case he regained consciousness.

I had been in the hospital emergency room for better than an hour before the counter transference occurred. For just a moment, I let my guard down. For just a moment, I thought, "Gee, this young boy is the same size and shape of my nephew, who was about the same age. Suddenly, it was as if I was watching an old, black and white horror movie. I watched as the boy's face changed. His face melted and twisted. He was no longer a stranger, but he was in fact my nephew. I knew what I was seeing was impossible, and that I was experiencing counter transference. But it still felt as if I got kicked in the stomach. I had to step away and catch my breath.

Those we serve in law enforcement may have similar experiences with counter transference in the day to day events of their job. They may not know about transference, and may need education from the Chaplain to explain this "normal reaction to an abnormal event".

When a law enforcement officer arrives on a scene with a dead body, there is an almost instantaneous evaluation of the scene. Our minds act like huge filing cabinets, and will automatically file what we see and experience in order of importance. Our minds will quickly try to filter and file the information. Subconsciously we will give the person that has been killed a certain value, to determine where this information will be filed in our brain. This is based on a "sliding scale". It's something totally unconscious, that each one of us does when faced with a similar situation. Our minds will kick in with this mental defense mechanism when facing a new situation that potentially can be extremely stressful. If the officer's mind gave a high amount of value to every critical incident scene, they would not be able to last long in their chosen career. Giving a high value in this situation would potentially bring on counter transference and would be debilitating for them. This value response is not one of being right or wrong; it is something that we all do as an automatic response.

Let me explain what is meant by an evaluation scale. When something bad happens to someone, we may give little emotional value to them, because we don't know the person, or we might think they deserve the trouble they are in because of their lifestyle, etc. On the other hand we may give it great deal of emotional value because the person involved was a friend or loved one or the person may be perceived as having a high degree of innocence.

When an officer arrives on the scene of a dead body, at a glance they begin processing the scene. This mental processing has sometimes been called a "Psychological

Autopsy". This is their first impression of what happened: a determination of what kind of a death the person died, who the person was, etc. The first consideration of the psychological autopsy is how the person died. Our subconscious mind quickly decides which of four kinds of death the person experienced:

Kind of Death

• Natural

• Accidental

• Suicide

• Homicide

With the kind of death the person experienced, there is an imputed lethality. What is meant by imputed lethality is how much a person has to do with their own death. An example of a high-imputed lethality would be a suicide, where a person purposely took their own life. A low imputed lethality might be a random shooting resulting in a homicide death. This is the second consideration of the psychological autopsy. The scale below shows Imputed Lethality:

Imputed Lethality Scale

High

Medium

Low

(*Scale measures implied lethality, i.e. the amount of a person's involvement in their own death.*)

(Suicide *would show high, while natural death would would show low*)

The third piece of the psychological autopsy, which is added to the kind of death and the imputed lethality; is the age, sex (male or female), innocence, and something called the value of the person:

- Age
- Sex
- Innocence
- Value

Value is determined by who the person is. Again, whether right or wrong, it is something that all of us do subconsciously. Consider for a moment which would hold more value for you of two teenagers – one was the captain of his football team, a straight "A" student, popular and loved by everyone, who has plans to become a missionary/doctor – the other is a high school drop-out, gang banger, who has been selling drugs to children and has spent time in and out of juvenile hall for various offenses. Even though we should not morally give one teen more value than the other, deep in our mind we still do it. So depending on how the officer perceives this body laying in front of him, will also determine the emotional and psychological impact it will have on him or her.

As an example of how an officer instantly processes a scene, imagine for a moment, a mother with her child at a park. She lost sight of her five year old daughter for what she thought would be just a couple of minutes, but then could not find her. After frantically searching for her daughter to no avail, she called the police. The police arrived very quickly and began searching for this little girl. One of the officers saw a child's shoe sticking out of some bushes. He opened the bushes, and was nearly overwhelmed with emotion. He had found the little girl. She had been horribly raped and then brutally strangled to death. Applying the psychological autopsy to this child, the officer found her death was by homicide, so her imputed lethality – her choice in the matter was totally not her own. She had no desire to die. Her age was young; she was a female; and very innocent looking. Her mother was apparently loving and would be devastated by this loss. Putting this together, the officer would give this child a great deal of value, and this would be a call that would be a great source of stress, and have a great psychological impact on his life. (29)

Law enforcement officers are often called to scenes involving suicides. They are unfortunately, a pretty widespread and common type of call. There are numerous reasons people commit suicide. Usually they have pain either real or imagined that is so unbearable that they think their only recourse is to end it all. This pain may be real or imagined. Harold Elliott broke down the requirements for someone to commit suicide. He says, "Over the years I've come to know that, in order for someone to commit suicide, at least two conditions must be met. First, there must be pain-physical, or more often mental. And second, there must be in the victim's mind a view that death is somehow benign, a state worth working toward-a state which the victim will be there, somehow to enjoy. They may picture it as oblivion-but an oblivion they will somehow "live" to enjoy." (30) He goes on to say, "For suicide to occur, the pain must be sufficient to overcome any potential negative perceptions of death" (31)

The ratios for suicides being attempted and completed are very different for the young versus the old. Among our population as a whole, the ratio of attempted to completed suicides is about 10 to one, i.e. 10 suicide attempts to one completion. For the young, the average is usually estimated to be around 100 attempts to one completion. For the elderly, who are not generally attempting to commit suicide for attention, or out of emotional outbursts, the ratio is generally 1 to 1. In other words, pretty much every elderly person that attempts suicide completes the attempt and dies. The elderly may find themselves dependent upon other people, lonely, depressed, or in difficult financial situations. Often they have the impression that they are being a burden and have already lived their life. A majority of suicide calls that an officer goes on will involve elderly people.

Any suicide is tragic, but an officer usually has good coping skills when the suicide involves an elderly person. They instantly assess the death when they arrive on scene, and one of the predominant features is the age. Going back to the psychological autopsy discussed earlier, the imputed lethality is high, and the age is elderly, which tends to lessen the appearance of innocence. On the other hand, if the suicide is involving a young person – a teen or even a pre-teen, the situation is quite different. The imputed lethality may still be high, but the officer may rationalize that the young person really didn't know what they were doing, or they were just trying to get attention and didn't really mean to kill themselves. The age is young (the younger the age, the higher the innocence level) causing the officer to be much more impacted by the call.

When working a suicide call as a Chaplain, one question is probably more frequently asked than others, even among those officers that don't consider themselves overly religious. They often ask, "Did they go to Hell for killing themselves?" This can be a difficult question to answer, without going into a religious diatribe. You may have different beliefs on the subject depending on your own religious background.

Historically, the idea that suicide is some sort of, or The unpardonable sin is more of a tradition than a church doctrine. In the early Christian Church, many Christians were surrendering themselves up to be thrown into the arena with lions in order to gain martyrdom. Saint Augustine was trying to stop this trend. He began teaching that suicide was an unpardonable sin, and people would go to Hell for doing it. This effectively stopped the martyrs, but did little to stem those who were miserable from committing suicide.

Chaplains are very often asked the question about Hell after a suicide. When I am asked, I normally say something to the effect that, "It is not how the person died that makes a difference where they spend eternity, but how they lived their life, and to whom they committed their life." We don't know what a person was thinking just before they died. They may have made peace with God a moment before death. We move in a world of time – of hours, minutes and seconds. God moves between the seconds.

The other common question is why a person committed suicide. Or people will start talking about the "If onlys". In other words, "If only I had been here." Or, "If only I hadn't yelled at them." And so on. Generally, a little probing reveals that the person was probably planning the suicide for some time. Most often I hear the person was very depressed, and suddenly seemed to get better. They got better because they had been wrestling with the idea of suicide and had finally made a decision. So even if the person had been there, it would have only put off the inevitable. It was not their fault, and they should not blame themselves.

In police work, depending on what part of the country you are in, there are a certain percentage of homicides an officer will have to deal with. These can be very stressful and very difficult to deal with psychologically. A particularly gruesome homicide scene can effect even the most hardened of officers.

A majority of law enforcement officers are mothers and fathers. If they are not parents, they probably have little brothers or sisters. Even if they are not parents, and don't have siblings, most all cops have a special love and compassion for children. Officers have big heroic hearts and the innocence of childhood – when corrupted by violence of any kind – can be especially traumatic and stressful for officers.

Certain types of calls in law enforcement work consistently bring stress to the officer because of their impact emotionally and potentially can lead to compassion fatigue, and Post Traumatic Stress Disorder (PTSD). At the top of the list is the line of duty death of someone they know, or from their department. A close second would be deaths and injuries of children in particular, or deaths of any person in general. They will be more or less severe depending on the value mentally assigned each death.

Moving down the list, other impacting critical incidents are personally threatening events, especially where the life of the officer or someone close to them is at risk; injury or death to operations personnel; knowing the victim; any grotesque sights, sounds, and smells from a scene; and a death of any officer in the department. The death of an officer will affect not only those that are close to him or her, but to an entire department, including sworn and non-sworn personnel. In today's society, an officer may work for several different agencies during the course of a career, so the impact is even more widely spread.

After repeatedly seeing traumatic scenes such as dead children, homicides, rapes, and other violent crimes, an officer will begin to develop a "trauma membrane" as a defense mechanism. J. Lindy describes this trauma membrane thusly, "Subsequent to trauma or disaster, victims begin to develop a psychological defense system that insulates them from continued intrusion or over-stimulation; however, it also insulates them from efforts by others to assist in their recovery. The membrane "thickens" with time, therefore early intervention after trauma or disaster is highly recommended." (32) Not only do these traumatic scenes cause severe stress for the officer, but the officer begins to build up walls that make it more difficult to reach them and help relieve this stress. This often leads to PTSD.

One of the most common sources of PTSD for a cop is officer involved shootings. There was an officer and his partner that were trying to make a routine stop. After a short distance, the suspect slowed to about 5 miles an hour, and finally pulled over to the side of the road. Just as the officers were stepping out, and preparing to approach the car, the driver put the car in reverse and rammed the officer's car, and tried to run down the other officer. The officer's partner was forced to shoot and kill the driver of the vehicle. Even though the officer driving the vehicle was not the shooter, he could remember every detail of the shooting months later.

Some of the symptoms of PTSD are nightmares, insomnia, vivid flashbacks of the incident, anxiety attacks, anger, concentration problems, depression, emotional detachment, and avoidance of people or certain areas that remind them of the incident.

Author Allen Kates discusses PTSD among law enforcement officers in his book "Cop Shock". Allen Kates says, "Regardless of whether cops at first satisfy the definition for PTSD or not, they sometimes develop the condition. They set themselves up for PTSD if they suppress their emotions after a traumatic incident and do not get proper support." (33) Officer's that suppress their emotions in this way often get "stuck" at that point, never recovering, or being able to move on. Life for them is changed. PTSD, if untreated, can eventually become totally debilitating, to the point that the officer can no longer continue being a cop.

Officers at a crime scene rarely show any emotions. They have been trained not to show emotion, and to control not only the situation, but also their own reactions. Even though they are not showing at the time, the reactions are there under the surface.

There have been many studies on PTSD among first responders. All of the studies find that there is a high amount of PTSD among law enforcement officers – much higher than in non-law enforcement occupations. Among all law enforcement officers, including present, former, and retired officers, Mann and Neece in their book "Workers' Compensation for Law Enforcement Related Post Traumatic Stress Disorder", estimate that there are 12 to 35 percent suffering from PTSD. (34) PTSD is even higher when you consider only those officers who have been involved in an officer involved shooting.

One particular kind of officer involved shooting is when a perpetrator forces the officer to shoot them. A special consideration needs to be well thought-out by the Chaplain for these officers who are involved in "victim precipitated homicides" (also known as "suicide by cop", "copicide", and other similar terms). Rebecca Stincelli, in an article entitled "Suicide by Cop: The Long Road Back", gives definitions to the various terms used in this phenomenon. She writes, "Suicide-by-cop: A colloquial term used to describe a suicidal incident whereby the suicidal subject engages in a consciously, life-threatening behavior to the degree that it compels a police officer to respond with deadly force." And, "Victim-precipitated homicide: A term which implies a shared responsibility between two (or more parties) whereby a suicidal subject provokes his or her own death by means of another." (35)

The commonly used term victim-precipitated homicide can be deceiving. It is very important for the chaplain to remember that the person who commits suicide by forcing a cop to shoot them is not a victim but a criminal. They have committed a crime by threatening the officer and by forcing the officer to kill them. Don't make the mistake of referring to the deceased as a victim.

There have been a number of studies in victim precipitated homicide. According to most of these studies, anywhere from 10-25% of officer involved shootings are considered to be suicide by cop. A study done in Los Angeles County shows some of the typical profile of a person that has completed a suicide by cop. This study shows:

96% of the perpetrators were male. Though women do occasionally choose this method of suicide, it is rare.

Ages ranged anywhere from 18-54 years.

Weapons ranged from firearms = 46%

knives and other stabbing instruments = 46%

fake firearms, or firearms replicas = 8%

58% asked the officer to kill them

58% had a psychiatric history

38% had attempted suicide on previous occasions

A full one half were intoxicated at the time

42% had a history of domestic violence

38% had a previous criminal history (36)

Law enforcement officers who have been forced into a victim-precipitated homicide are very likely to have a lot of stress, and second-guessing about their actions. Louise C. Pyers, MS, wrote a paper regarding law enforcement assisted suicide. Pyers said, "Police officers reacting to the aftermath of "suicide by cop" display symptoms of post-traumatic stress disorder, which adversely affects their ability to perform their duties. Police officers are also victims in these cases. Hyper vigilance, fear, anger, sleeplessness, and depression are among the many symptoms reported. In many instances, the timing, speed at which the encounter escalated and officer's perception of immediate danger to self or others left him or her with no choice but to use deadly force. Yet, second guessing on the part of the officer is common." (37) The exception to this is if the perpetrator of suicide by cop was attempting to hurt or did actually do harm to an officer, or a civilian. In this kind of situation, the officer has a much easier time reconciling his actions to himself, because he was defending a fellow officer, or an innocent civilian.

A suicide by cop is always going to be a critical incident to all of the officers involved. When given a choice, most officers will not shoot. Often times, television and movie cops are portrayed as heroic when they kill all the bad guys. A line from the story from Dateline NBC called "Suicide cops: in the line of duty", puts it very well. It said, "Most cops don't kill people – but when they do, they aren't always made to feel heroic." (38) As a matter of fact, in most instances of suicide by cop, the officers will try to save the life of the perpetrator after they shoot them.

There was a particular criminal, attempting to kidnap a teenage girl. He hit her in the back of the head with a big metal flashlight, and drug her into his car. After a while, he couldn't get the bleeding to her head to stop, and released her. She got a good description of his car, and the license plate. When the perpetrator was pulled over, he got out of his car and got into a crouching position as if he was going to shoot at the officer's. They shot him, but it turned out he had nothing but a cell phone. Here is how the Sacramento Bee described what an eyewitness said happened next, "The officers who shot Robertson immediately tore his clothes off and applied bandages to his wounds." (39) They were trying to keep him from bleeding to death. Immediately after the shooting, the Sacramento Bee quoted the perpetrator as saying "I need to die. I'm a bad person. Thanks for shooting me." (40)

Just as there are countless reasons a person may attempt to commit suicide, there are numerous reasons they choose to try to involve law enforcement officers in their decision to take their life. There are two common emotions that can be linked to practically every suicide by cop. They are depression and rage. When you put the two of these together, you have a formula for disaster. Hal Brown, LICSW says, "People who are very angry in addition to being depressed are more likely to involve others in their suicide. When a person ends his life in front of the news cameras, they want to send the message "I'll show you"; to a lover who jilted them, a company that fired them, or a society that they believe never gave them a chance. Some people stage elaborate suicides solely for the benefit of the one person they set up to find them." (41)

Some suicidal people choose suicide by cop, because they don't see any other options. They may be elderly, or may not have ready access to an easy means of ending their lives. These people may not be angry at all, but simply looking to the law enforcement officer to help them end their misery. They may see the officer as doing them one last final service.

Of course there are also those that are truly mentally ill. We could probably also lump in this category those in a mental haze from drug abuse. These individuals may have had multiple dealings with law enforcement officers, and have no fear of the officer's gun. They may see death as an escape, or be so deranged as to simply not care. Their judgment may be so impaired that they don't understand that the officer will use deadly force to protect themselves, and those around them if they feel there is a threat of mortal danger.

Some people are desperate, and want to leave whether they live or die in someone else's hand. They may think thoughts like, "I am not really sure I want to die, so I will pull a gun on a cop and see what happens, whether I live or die." In this category may also be the petty criminal, who out of desperation begins to take chances, like daytime robberies. They may think something like, "I am either going to score really big, or I am going to die trying."

The least common, but certainly the most devastating suicides by cop involve other law enforcement officers. This occurs when a cop, usually on suspension or recently retired, seems to have something snap in their heads. They may have deep resentment, hurt and anger against the department. In addition they may be deeply depressed, and seemingly without a way out. The officers that are involved in this kind of suicide by cop are especially traumatized, and will have a deep sense of guilt for a very long time.

Suicide by cop, in whatever form it takes, will always take its toll on the officers involved. They will experience critical incident stress, and the event may haunt their mind, thoughts and dreams for a long while.

After any kind of officer involved shooting, the officer's gun will be taken away. The gun will be needed for forensics, etc. The officer will be put on administrative leave, or given a desk job until after an investigation is done. Up until recent years, nearly all agencies would automatically take an officer's gun, without giving them a replacement. More and more agencies have seen the importance of getting a replacement gun for the officer involved in an officer involved shooting, so this doesn't happen as often as it once did.

An officer's gun is like an extension of who they are, just like their badge. Al Benner, a psychologist that serves many of the NYPD, was interviewed by NBC's Dateline regarding officer involved shootings. Benner said that taking away an officer's gun after a shooting is a potential death sentence for the officer. (42) Keith Bettinger says, "Psychological harm can be done if the officer is sent home unarmed. It raises questions of doubt in the officer's mind. He wonders if the department suspects him of wrongdoing, or doubts his capabilities as an officer." (43) It can be an added stress if the agency the officer works for is one that doesn't have a policy to replace an officer's gun after a shooting.

The other side of officer involved shootings is officer's who are killed in the line of duty. According to the American Police Hall of Fame, an average of one law enforcement officer is killed in the line of duty in the United States every 57 hours. Most of these officers are killed with firearms, and in particular hand guns. Between the years of 1976 and 1998, there were over 1,800 officers killed in the line of duty. (44)

A line of duty death will cause the officer in an agency to be aware of their own mortality. The men and women who worked with the fallen officer, "experience a grief that few civilians truly understand. A line of duty death impacts the agency or department to its very core." (45) If the officers are not provided an outlet to express their emotions, such as a debriefing, or a CISM, (CISMs discussed in more detail in section three) they may suppress their grief. "Suppressing grief may cause them to doubt their self-worth as a community servant or, worse yet, question whether anyone appreciates the risks they take and the need they have to be the professional they are." (46) Line of duty deaths can cause stress throughout the department, and can affect countless officers.

Another stress from police work is a fairly modern phenomenon. With the advent of the spread of AIDS, there is always an underlying fear of getting a needle stick when patting down a suspect. Immediately after getting stuck by a needle, an officer's mind may think the very worst. In reality, there is a much greater chance of getting hepatitis than AIDS from a dirty needle.

Of course, precautions need to be immediately taken if an officer is stuck by a needle. The first step is to help the officer remain calm and in control. Most often the immediate reaction is panic, followed closely by anger. According to Dwight A. Polk, MSW and paramedic program coordinator, the following steps need to be taken, "Wounds should be immediately washed with warm, soapy water, if available. If in a field environment, cleanse the area with alcohol or commercial hand cleaner. If the injury is the result of needle stick, drawing a circle around the site will help to identify the area for later examination. If needed, dress the wound to prevent further contamination. Mucous membranes or eyes should be flushed immediately with copious amounts of water." (47)

There is a real risk of being exposed to AIDS in law enforcement work, and often just the awareness of this reality is stressful to a cop.

The criminal justice system is yet another major source of stress for law enforcement officers. Often the criminal justice system is perceived as inefficient, and pro-criminal. "Officers complain of court rulings perceived as too lenient on offenders; court rulings perceived as too restrictive on methods of criminal suppression and investigation; perceived premature release of offenders on bail, probation, or parole; inconveniently scheduled court appearances and long waits before testifying; lack of follow-up with police to tell them how cases turned out; perceived lack of respect from judges, lawyers, and others in the criminal justice system..." (48)

Some officers express intense frustration and stress with making arrests, only to see cases dismissed, or plea bargained away. Some officers feel their hands are being tied, restricting them from making a difference on their patrol, and reducing crime in their city. They may begin to feel a lack of accomplishment as they see people who they arrested just days earlier, back on the streets, and involved in the same criminal activities that got them arrested in the first place.

Overlapping the frustration and stress from the criminal justice system is the shift work that most officers work. The court system doesn't work on a rotating shift. Often times an officer may work a late shift, getting off duty a short time before he or she has to appear in court to testify. The officer may be exhausted from a long night, and feel ready to do nothing more than just climb into bed and pull the covers over their head. Instead, they have to go toe to toe, and match wits with the public defender's office.

Law enforcement officers take their work very seriously. When they arrest a suspect of whom they are certain committed a crime, they will try to make sure that all of the evidence is "uncontaminated", and pure. They will gather their evidence, interview witnesses, and try to present a strong case. No matter how strong their case, it is still up to the prosecutor to take the case to court and convince a judge and jury of a suspect's guilt. There are times when, real or perceived, the suspected criminals have their charges dismissed because of a poor presentation by the prosecuting attorney.

There are many officers that see the court system as their greatest source of stress, and frustration. When the defense attorney suggests evidence contamination, or inept police work, the whole department can be effected. For an example we could look at the widespread condemnation of the Los Angeles Police department a few years ago after the now infamous Rodney King beating and the televised O.J. Simpson trial. The whole country watched over and over as officers beat Rodney King with their night sticks – and as OJ Simpson tried on the "bloody gloves that didn't fit". This segways into the fourth major stressor in law enforcement, which comes as a result of the general public and the media.

The public and the media have a close bond. The media tends to feed off of public opinion, while the media try's to shape that same public opinion. Media depends on the general public for ratings, and thus how much money they get, while the public depends on the media for entertainment, news, and information.

Law enforcement in our country has only been trying to have a mutually beneficial relationship with the media for about the last thirty-five years. Many larger law enforcement agencies have set up public relations departments, or put in place public information officers (PIOs) as spokespeople for the department. PIOs are usually well trained officers, with a knowledge of, or background in media. Generally, the PIOs suggest news stories to the media, give statements and interviews at crime scenes, and respond to press inquiries.

This doesn't mean that everything is now mutually satisfactory with the relationship between the media and law enforcement. There are still periods of strained relations. "The relationship between law enforcement agencies and the print and electronic media fluctuates between mutual hostility and admiration. Historically, the admiration cycle between the two professions is short lived!" (49)

The two driving forces of mass media are competition (with other news outlets) and profit. "The primary motivation for a large percentage of these type of organizations is to find ways to tell a story in a compelling and accurate way, or to take the easier way out by debunking traditional values and institutions, reveling in the exposed clay feet of public figures, or seeking a controversial aspect in every story, or social issue, as a means to achieve an audience. This leads to greater recognition or profits." (50) Some people, especially those in media, would argue that they are just giving the public what they want, or that the arts are "merely a mirror reflection of society". This argument falls far short as "an attempt to justify the scarcity of noble intentions by some of the people in this industry." (51)

This reckless approach of trying to get a controversial story often leads to an exploitive and even a hostile attitude towards those in law enforcement. This seems to especially be the case, (though surely not limited to), some of the fringe type media people, who are not directly employed by a reputable media agency. These self-employed media types call themselves freelancers, and get paid by the job. Here is an example of free-lance work, "An officer, on riot duty, becomes separated from his squad at a violent demonstration and is attacked by two men armed with make-shift clubs. He defends himself appropriately with non-lethal force but is photographed by a journalist at a moment in which it seems that the officer is brutalizing one of his assailants who is on the ground and appears to the camera's eye, to be unarmed and helpless. The next day, the front page of the newspaper has that photo splashed sensationally across it. Over the next few days, the officer is forced to explain and defend his actions to his superiors, family and friends." (52) An officer apparently beating a helpless suspect sells more newspapers, than an officer defending himself. With distorted press accounts such as this, the officer's stress level is raised as their concern for not ending up on the news affects them at every major crime scene.

Many officers have offered that they are resentful of their work being criticized or distorted by the media. Some also see the news media as focusing too much on the rights of the criminal, and not enough on the results of their criminal actions, or the harm done to victims and officers. The last few years, there have been more lawsuits brought against law enforcement officers by citizens, often after a particularly skewed picture or piece of video presented by the media. This at times leads to an officer being unsure of how to do their job. They may feel a certain level of force is called for, they may second-guess themselves over a fear of lawsuits because of the presence of media, and therefore use less force than the situation requires. They may put themselves and those around them in grave danger by doing this.

One major contributor to inaccurate or distorted news reporting comes from a "You saw it here first," mentality. Many news agencies think that quality lies in breaking the news before their competitor, rather than in presenting an unbiased presentation of the facts. With the advent of bloggers, and instant internet news, it becomes more and more of a challenge to get the story out quickly. Not to mention cell phones with camera and video capabilities. A note to the Chaplain is necessary here. If you are asked to make, or assist in making a death notification for an officer killed in the line of duty, it is imperative you get to the family as quickly as possible. You need to be there before the media is able to flash gruesome scenes of someone's loved one all over the television. The actual process of delivering a death notification can be found in section IV, the Chaplain's role.

Many officers complain about how the newspaper, or television news just can't seem to get the story right. Several have told me that they have stopped watching the news, and reading the paper because it is often so inaccurate. It is frustrating for them to have been on the scene of a crime, and then to hear a story that sounds so different from what actually happened that they almost think they are talking about two different crime scenes.

Not all newscasters and media types are hurtful to law enforcement. Some genuinely want to help, and can be very useful in putting out the selective information that the department wants reported. This is usually done by the PIO. However, building a good working relationship with the media takes hard work, and dedication. There is not a lot of trust between members of the news agencies and law enforcement. "The print media views law enforcement with great caution, sensitive to the role they play as the "watchdog" of government and ever-mindful that law enforcement can trample all over the Constitution unless carefully monitored by zealous reporters." (53) Officers are also well aware that no matter what their agency does to foster good will among those in broadcast and print journalism, they will attack, bite, and undermine the officer if they feel it is in their best interest to do so to sell papers, or get ratings.

The general public will usually fall in line with the attitude of the news media. If most of the news media love their officers, and paint them as local heroes, much of the general public will think the same thing. If the media portrays them as bigots, and bullies, once again much of the general public will fall in line right behind them.

Of course, many people don't need the media to teach them to not like, or trust law enforcement. Many people learn to hate cops from the time they are very young from their own parents. They grow up hating and distrusting the police, and it comes through in their attitudes. When a parent says something like "Oh, great! There's a cop driving behind me." It sends a message to their children that "Cops are out to get you, so you had better watch out!"

Street cops are often taught to distrust the general public as well. Here is an example of what many a rookie cop's early contact with the public is like. "A rookie officer tells his fellow officers about having an obscene "message" gouged into the paint across the side of his new car in its parking spot at home. The nature of the words makes it clear that the vandal(s) know the owner of the car is a policeman. His fellow officers all are quick to tell similar stories and the rookie doesn't feel any less angry as he phones his insurance agent." (54) Is it any wonder that law enforcement officers begin to distrust people early on in their careers?

It's ironic that the average person on the street expects the cop to be there when he or she needs them, but to look the other way while they commit a crime, such as DUI, smoking marijuana, or speeding. The officer is expected to take whatever criticism, hostility, ignorance or apathy that is directed toward them, and still maintain public approval.

It can be even worse for the officer's family. The jokes start to fly about not doing certain things around "her" because her husband is a cop. Or, kids may dare the son or daughter of an officer to skip school. They then make fun of them saying they won't do it because their Mom or Dad is a cop. This kind of treatment contributes to the social isolation the officer already feels, and draws them deeper into the "us vs. them" mentality.

The last major stressor law enforcement officers have to deal with has more to do with the officer's personal life, and how they individually deal with stress.

Cops see the seamier side of life, while their friends and family who are not in law enforcement, don't even realize that other world exists. Just like most other civilians, they never see it. The officer may even begin to get a feeling of superiority to the general public because of this knowledge. The problem is the officer's are actually losing "real world" wisdom. They don't realize the world is not primarily made up of criminals and fools but of decent and kind folks, who are contributing members to society.

Almost the polar opposite of those who fear, and hate law enforcement officers, are what might be called "cop groupies". These people (usually female but there are males as well) will seek to have extramarital affairs with officers. They are attracted by the uniform, the authority and power it represents, or some combination.

The psychological makeup of a law enforcement officer tends to paint him or her as a thrill seeker. Their psychological makeup leads them to experiment, search out and seek for adventures. This tendency to take risks, often leads them to sexual infidelity.

Many groupies have an unhealthy level of attraction to cops. Some become obsessed with them. They will seek out relationships, and offer sexual favors with law enforcement officers. As retired Police Chief Chuck Pratt put it, "It is extremely hard for anyone to avoid "adventures" when attractive members of the opposite sex are openly, persistently inviting." (55)

When you put this together you have:

1.   An officer's desire for adventure

2.   People that are searching for sexual relationships with officers

3.   Officers may be working a beat that is far from home

4.   Little chance of his or her getting caught

5.   They are often working late hours, after dark

You end up with a very strong temptation to cheat. If the officer gives in to the temptation, especially if he or she is married, this creates a huge stressor in their life. The guilt from committing these acts will lead to an enormous well of guilt. According to retired Police Chief Chuck Pratt, often these sexual infidelities with these so called cop groupies, are directly linked to the high divorce rate among law enforcement officers. (56)

This doesn't mean that law enforcement officers are going to "jump in the sack" with every woman that gives them a second glance. However the Chaplain needs to be aware that the temptation is out there, and is very real. Unfortunately, it can also be directed at the Chaplain who works with, and may dress and act similar to a cop. Some will be allured simply by the authority the Chaplain seems to wield. Beware Chaplains!

Many times, the temptation to commit adultery is much more subtle than someone walking up and saying "Hey, how about a roll in the hay?" The officer may be true to his wife, and have no intentions of ever having an affair. He may not see himself as the kind of person who would have an affair. In fact, the encounter may start out completely innocent. A woman may express an interest in his job, or some stressor he has recently encountered on his job, or even something stressful going on at home. A conversation takes place that is mutually supportive and friendly. The officer may not give it a whole lot of thought, other than to think about how nice it was to talk to someone who genuinely listened, and was interested in what they had to say. They may have a sense that "she was a really nice person". No activity, other than talking takes place. However, over time more conversations take place, and with each conversation, more information is shared. Intimate thoughts and feelings may come out, and secrets may be passed back and forth. In that instant, whether the officer himself realizes it or not, he is involved in what has been called an "affair of the heart". This relationship is sucking away much of his energy and passion that should be reserved for his wife. For all intents and purposes, aside from the physical part of the relationship, he is in the middle of an affair. The physical part of the relationship will not be far behind. As the connection is made mentally, there is an attraction that develops. At first it may just be that the officer considers her "nice to be around". However as the mental intimacy builds, it builds toward physical intimacy. The final result – the affair has occurred.

We have established that being a cop is a very stressful job. The typical officer will also have the normal stressors faced by everyone else such as poor health or the illness of a loved one. They may have relationship problems; the stress of buying a new home; the birth of children, etc. How an officer deals with stress in his or her home life will probably be the same way they handle stress when they are on the job. If they try to mask it, or ignore it, stress doesn't go away. If they cram it down, it will eventually explode. Some officers will try to drown their stress with alcohol. All of these unhealthy ways of handling stress only contribute to the problem. They do not reduce or eliminate the stress in their lives.

There are five major sources of stress for an officer as we have discussed in this chapter:

1.   Stressors from the Law Enforcement Organization itself.

2.   Stressors from doing the job.

3.   Working with the criminal justice system.

4.   Stressors from Media and the public.

5.   The officer's personal life.

How an officer handles stress will directly relate to their job performance. When an officer is recruited into the academy, the agency carefully screens for any mental defects that may cause problems in the future. They make sure the officer is mentally fit and up to the challenge of Police work. After academy, in most agencies there is little mentioned about mental health, and where an officer is emotionally. This indifference over the course of a career often leads an officer down a path that leads to divorce, alcohol abuse, depression, and at its worst, suicide.

CHAPTER 4
THE ONSET OF MORAL DECAY AND CYNICISM

The path we have examined in the past few chapters has mapped how the average law enforcement officer seems to be malevolently led from being altruistic to a state of cynicism. Many experts say they can actually detect the first signs of cynicism as far back as the police academy. This grand figure of integrity, and morality -- this honorable person who wanted no more than "to make a difference" -- this modern day Paladin with a shield on their chest, and their weapon at their side-- has traveled down this path to cynicism with little resistance, virtually unaware of the journey. They walk without complaint, ignorant of the consequences, as a sheep to the slaughter.

The experiences an officer endures over the course of a career in law enforcement can and will have an effect on them. The various stressors will wear on them, pounding away at their armor. The images of death and depravity; the sounds that the victims make, and their silent screams etched upon their lifeless faces; the smell of death, and the lowest depths of depravity to which humanity can fall, all grind away at their minds. When they lay their heads on their pillows to sleep, do the images of what they have seen come rushing into their memory like a flood? For many, they do.

Sometimes we forget the law enforcement officer is not more than human. Society may forget, or never realize that cops are not immune to the horrors, conflicts, and miseries – the depravity and indignities they have to face every day. Their world is one of criminals and victims. They see the very worst of society, but rarely its beauty. Chaplains have the opportunity to point out the beauty that they may otherwise never see. We can point out the lovely, the worthy, and the innocent.

Many in psychological circles talk about the flight or fight instinct. We as people have a makeup to either face an opponent, or run away to fight another day. We may also posture, (make ourselves look bigger and tougher than we are) or submit to a stronger opponent in hopes that they will not hurt us. Officers on duty don't have the luxury of typical human responses such as fight or flight. That decision is taken away from them as soon as they put on the badge and strap on their gun. No matter how badly they may want to run away and hide, or submit, their training and integrity forces them to face the danger staring them in the eye.

After an officer has had all he or she can stand, and they can no longer endure the stress and pressure, they will probably call in sick. They may think of it as a mental health day, which probably isn't that far from the truth. They may even take some time off to try and work through the pain they are feeling in their psyche. The problem with just taking time off is they eventually have to go back to work and face their pain.

The normal human response to cumulative stress is to eventually reach a breaking point, where they can take no more, and finally collapse. If an officer continues to live under stress, as most do, without making any changes to relieve the stress, the stress will continue to work. It will affect them detrimentally in all three components of their being; physically, mentally, and spiritually.

We are all triune beings, i.e. we are all comprised with three parts to our being. We are as much spiritual beings, as we are physical, and emotional. The ancient Greeks were the great thinkers of their time. They were often the doctors, teachers and philosophers. The Greeks broke down the human persona to describe the three distinct components. The first component is the "Soma", which is defined as the body apart from the soul. The Soma has physical attributes including form and the senses including hearing, sight, taste, touch and smell.   The second component is the "Psyche", which includes the mind, will and emotions. This is where a person's personality resides. The last piece of the trinity that makes us who we are is the "pneuma", which can be translated breathe, or wind. It vividly paints the picture of God breathing life into us, as he did with Adam, the first man.   The pneuma is our very essence; the spiritual part of us, where we have our character and our integrity.   It is the pneuma whence comes our morality and our ethics.

Often times, people will try to "feed" one portion of who they are, to the detriment of the other two. They may feed their lusts and desires, showing little or no restraint as they lead a life meant to satisfy their physical and emotional appetites. They may have little regard for the spiritual part of their being, and have no qualms about committing crimes or hurting people to get what they want. The Bible describes this state of not having a conscience in I Timothy 4:2, "Speaking lies in hypocrisy; having their conscience seared with a hot iron..."

Officers going down the path of cynicism may find themselves ignoring their conscience - that still small voice that is within every one of us, pleading with them to make right choices. Instead they continue choosing to make poor decisions against their moral judgment. Or they may cram their emotions so tightly within, that their emotions nearly suffocate. While still others will push their bodies and minds beyond the limits that they were meant to endure, going with very little sleep, and another cup of coffee, or energy drink.

Daniel A. Goldfarb, PhD describes police work in this fashion, "Life is like an airplane. An airplane has four forces working on it. Gravity pulls it down. But the wings can produce lift, which picks it up. The engines produce thrust. But the air around the plane produces drag or resistance. In order to fly a pilot will take the plane, point it into the greatest amount of resistance (into the wind), and add the maximum amount of thrust. Maximum thrust into maximum resistance produces lift. Once airborne your height or elevation is controlled by attitude. If you pull back on the stick the nose of the plane points up. You have a positive attitude and will climb. If you push the stick forward you have a negative attitude and will fall. Fall far enough and you will crash." (57) He goes on with his analogy to say, "The problem with cynicism is that it destroys all attitude. All attitude becomes negative and thus the cynic will eventually crash. Cops more than people in any other profession are in continual danger of becoming cynics. In continual danger of crashing!" (58)

Cynicism goes deeper than just the mind of the officer. It goes beyond the body, where it may be causing ulcers, stiff muscles and joints, and fatigue. It reaches in, with its long bony fingers, and claws its way into the spiritual part of who they are. It begins to ferment, and putrefy in a cop's spirit, and rots away their moral integrity. It becomes rancid deep in their inner most being, and begins to control them. The decisions they make, and even their physical body will begin to show signs of weakness.

The officer may see the person they are when no one else is around, and realize they no longer like who they are becoming. But it becomes very difficult to lance the wound and release the poison of cynicism once it gets down deep into their spirit.

Without divine intervention, it may seem they have gone beyond the point of no return. Is there hope for them? Press on dear reader.

SECTION II
COMPROMISE OF CHARACTER

CHAPTER 5
LIKE A SCARECROW IN A MELON PATCH

Jeremiah 10: 5 *"Like a scarecrow in a melon patch, their idols cannot speak; they must be carried because they cannot walk. Do not fear them; they can do no harm nor can they do any good."* (1)

It is fitting to start this section on the hidden pain of law enforcement officers, with a verse from the writings of Jeremiah.   Aside from Job, no Old Testament person suffered more than Jeremiah.   Much of his suffering was physical as he worked in the office of a prophet, condemning the people for their wrong doing. The people would often abuse him because of his preaching, and even threw him in a foul dungeon, where he was up to his armpits in slime.

Jeremiah suffered a great deal psychologically as even his own family turned against him. Jeremiah is known as the weeping prophet, not so much because of the physical persecution he was forced to endure, but because of the mental and emotional anguish in his soul.

Jeremiah used the figure of the scarecrow to demonstrate how lifeless and powerless the idols were that the people worshipped.   The scarecrow served to keep birds from eating up and destroying the crops of the Israelites.   On the outside the scarecrow really looked impressive, with its scary face, and upraised arms to frighten away ignorant birds from the melon patch. On the inside however, the scarecrow was hollow and lifeless.

Many law enforcement officers over time become pessimistic, distrustful of everyone and cynical. They look fine from the outside, just like the scarecrow. Their uniform is always immaculate, pressed and neat, and their shoes are always polished. They have become very good at putting on a disguise every morning to hide the fact that they are hollow, and hurting inside. Most people the officer comes in contact with will be fooled by the masks they wear. They can put on an appearance that says everything is under control. They appear tough enough to handle anything life passes their way. If you ask them, they will tell you they are doing fine. But on the inside, they are anything but okay.

It takes a lot of work to overcome a negative tendency. It is much easier to just give in to it. Tendencies can be positive or negative. Every one of us has normally occurring tendencies, whether promoted by our work, personality, upbringing, our religious faith, or our genetic makeup. We decide regularly whether we will give in to these tendencies, or resist them. Law enforcement work, as has been seen in section one, encourages certain tendencies towards cynicism, stress reactions, divorce, alcohol and drug abuse, and suicide. Enough officers end up with these specific symptoms, that a real pattern of behavior can easily be distinguished. Nearly every officer who makes a career out of law enforcement will end up with at least a degree of distinguishable cynicism.

Stress is a major factor working against an officer. It can be charted over the course of a career. "Stress typically affects the behavior of officers along a continuum that can include (a) underlying stress not yet manifested in outward effects, (b) mid-level stress, manifested in such ways as excessive drinking or an unacceptably high number of discourtesy complaints, and (c) debilitating stress, resulting in inadequate job performance, severe health problems, or suicide."(2) This kind of stress can have a number of damaging physical and emotional effects on officers. They may vary from person to person in intensity, but they all will have some level or degree of stress symptoms. Some of the symptoms include suspiciousness, emotional detachment, PTSD, heart problems including heart attacks, ulcers, weight gain, reduced efficiency in performing duties, reduced self esteem and morale, excessive aggressiveness, marital or other relationship and family issues, such as extramarital affairs, divorce, or domestic violence, absenteeism, early retirement, and ultimately suicide. (3)

Daniel A. Goldfarb Ph.D. puts the subject of the effects of stress on law enforcement in a very striking way. Dr. Goldfarb relates stress directly to an officer's badge when he says, "Perhaps it weighs only 2 ounces overall. Large ones may run to 4 ounces. But when that badge is pinned on, there is a weight unknown to most law enforcement officers. The true weight of the badge is not overcome by muscle, not found in the gym, not measured on a scale. This weight requires a strength and conditioning for which few officers are trained. The badge is not just pinned on a chest, it is pinned on a lifestyle. The heaviness of the badge makes the law enforcement officer different from other professionals." (4)

The chronic stress an officer endures over the course of a career will affect him or her in two distinct ways. Prolonged stress causes the average person to regress. They will tend to become more immature, and childish. People tend to naturally regress psychologically during chronic discomfort. The other effect of chronic stress on officers is they become numb, or immune to the sensitivity of other people. "They can't stand to continually see human misery. They must stop feeling or they won't survive. The mind has this defense mechanism so people can continue working in horrible situations. If they kept their normal sensitivity, they would fall apart. As they become insensitive to their own suffering, they become insensitive to the suffering of others. When treated with indignity they lose not only a sense of their own dignity but also the dignity of others. The pain of others stops bothering them, and they are no longer bothered when they hurt others." (5)

There is evidence that long-term cumulative stress may be a major contributor to cancer. "In one study, researchers found that people who reported they had suffered from workplace problems over a 10-year period had more than five times the risk of colorectal cancer as those who reported no workplace problems, even when diet and other risk factors were the same."(6) "Animal studies show that rats subjected to stress undergo DNA changes in the cells of their livers that if unchecked could lead to cancer-causing mutations. Other studies show that stressed animals are more susceptible to cancer-causing substances in the environment." (7) Aside from causing cancer, stress can cause a weakened immune system, which can lead to a number of health problems. "Stress is thought to weaken the immune system. A strong immune system is needed to destroy damaged cells that could lead to cancer." (8)

Different people use different methods to try to relieve stress. Some choose healthy alternatives, such as strenuous exercise, while others choose alcohol or drugs to try to numb their pain and stress. I have had officers tell me they drink to forget, and to numb the pain. "For a civilian the physical effects of addiction are enough to cause an early death. In Law Enforcement we add many factors to our chances of an early demise. The conditions and environment in which we work demand us to be emotionally, mentally, and physically alert. When we are in the depths of addiction we cannot sense or perceive the situations around us. That mechanism that seems built into us which signals a warning or alarm isn't working or worse is sending us false information. This not only jeopardizes us but also the people we work with and the persons we are sworn to protect." (9) Alcohol use (not necessarily alcoholism) has been found to be a significant factor in most suicides committed by cops. They tend to use the alcohol to help them gain the courage to take their own life, or to numb themselves before committing suicide.

I have responded to several officer suicides over my career as a Chaplain, and every one of them involved excessive alcohol use.

There is a great deal of supporting statistical data relating to law enforcement officers with drinking problems. Among the general population, about 10% of those who drink become alcoholics. If you pull out just the segment of population that are law enforcement officers, the number of people who will become alcoholics jumps up to 23 percent.

An officer may have a tendency to compartmentalize bad behavior. This is especially true of male officers, though their female counterparts may also do this. Men in general have a predisposition to this kind of behavior. The male brain has been described as resembling a waffle, with numerous squares or compartments. Each part of their life has its own compartment, or box. When they watch television, they are in their television box. When they are having a conversation, they are in their conversation box. The male brain doesn't do well in mixing the boxes, and can only really be in one box at a time. The officer may think that their drinking, or drug use, or whatever their vice is not a big deal because it is only one small box or part of who they are, and it doesn't interfere with other parts of who they are.

The tendency to compartmentalize bad behavior does not excuse it. The definition of Integrity is "whole, entire, and complete". The root word is integer and is used for a whole number i.e. not a fraction. When we divide up our lives, and try to justify bad behavior in this way it makes us a "fractional" person, and a fractional person doesn't have integrity. James 1:8 tells us a double-minded person is unstable in all their ways. We need to challenge officers to live a life of integrity – to stand apart from the crowd as people of integrity. We need to challenge them to live their lives the same way in front of people as they do when no one is looking.

Officers will often put up walls to protect themselves. Male officers especially, will try to never show emotion, or tell anyone when they are hurting. They will try to keep up appearances that nothing is wrong. But just like the scarecrow in Jeremiah 10, they may be empty inside -- their ability to deal with life and their career may be spent and they may feel all used up inside.

CHAPTER 6
PTSD AND COMPASSION FATIGUE – HAUNTED OFFICERS NEEDING HELP

One Christmas my parents gave me a "Creepy Crawlers Bug Maker" kit. It was great fun. I could take this "Mad Scientist's plasti-goop" and make all kinds of creatures by simply squirting the "goop" into the special molds. You put the mold in the special oven and baked them. Then I could put stickers on them or paint them anyway I wanted.

Wouldn't it be nice if we could make heroes that easily? Obviously it would be more challenging than using the Mad Scientist's black goo and a baking mold. How do you suppose we would make one? What would be the secret formula that could transform a person from "zero to hero" like in the comic books? Perhaps we would require a person who wanted to become a hero to personally gather up specific items. The ingredient list might look something like this:

- One tear from a Nile crocodile.
- Pull a tooth from a Great White Shark.
- A cup of snow from the very top of Mount Everest.
- Pluck a whisker from a roaring Siberian Tiger.
- Collect a drop of lava from the center of Mauna Loa, Hawaii, the world's largest active volcano.
- Make Chuck Norris cry, and steal the tear from his cheek.

- Add a tablespoon of blazing hot sauce for flavor, and stir vigorously.

There is no such thing as a chemical potion to make a hero. Even if there were, how would we know we were successful? How do we know a hero when we see one? Perhaps a better question is -- what makes a hero?

There are many kinds of heroes. Our society honors heroes with awards for bravery and courage, among others. We salute their self sacrificing work in charitable contribution in our communities. Sometimes they are members of our own families. But, if you ask a person recognized as a hero if they are one, the answer will always be, "No". They don't think they have done anything special. This leads us to see one of the true ingredients of a hero --- humility. A true hero doesn't look for personal recognition.

A Harris Poll was conducted in August of 2001 asking 1,022 people to "name people they thought of as heroes, *without reviewing a list or having any names suggested to them.*" Overwhelmingly the number one answer was JESUS CHRIST. Several named their Father or Mother as their hero.

Many reasons were given for why certain people were heroes. Below are a handful of the most common reasons cited in no particular order:

- "Not giving up until the goal is accomplished"
- "Doing what's right regardless of personal consequences"
- "Willingness to risk personal safety to help others"
- "Staying level-headed in a crisis"

A certain widow woman was brought to the attention of President Abraham Lincoln. He was told she had lost her five sons during the Civil War. Later it turned out she had lost two sons, but the eloquence of his letter to her remains a great example to us. It reads,

"Dear Madam: I have been shown in the files of the War Department a statement of the Adjutant-General of Massachusetts that you are the mother of five sons who have died gloriously on the field of battle. I feel how weak and fruitless must be any words of mine which should attempt to beguile you from the grief of a loss so overwhelming. But I cannot refrain from tendering to you the consolation that may be found in the thanks of the Republic they died to save. I pray that our heavenly Father may assuage the anguish of your bereavement, and leave you only the cherished memory of the loved and lost, and the solemn pride that must be yours to have laid so costly a sacrifice upon the altar of freedom.

Yours very sincerely and respectfully,

A. Lincoln." (As quoted from Freerepublic.com)

The list of reasons cited above to consider someone a hero most certainly fit our brave men and women who put their life at risk everyday while protecting our communities.

So what makes a hero? Hopefully by the time you finish reading this book you will have a much better idea.

Many law enforcement officers have a second career as a reserve military person. Many have given their lives serving their country over-seas. Many coming back have PTSD or other issues from the war.

There is a common challenge for career law enforcement officers to be discussed in this chapter. PTSD is a very real issue that many of them live with. Post Traumatic Stress Disorder, or PTSD, is very common among law enforcement officers. Many experts say that up to 30% of officers suffer from PTSD.

If PTSD is common among cops, compassion fatigue is the issue that affects, or will affect most career chaplains. We will cover both of these ailments in this chapter. A number of officers have told me, if you work in law enforcement long enough, you will develop PTSD. There are specific signs and symptoms to be aware of.

To better understand what PTSD is, it's important to understand the components that make up the disorder. Here are some expert definitions of these terms from Jeffrey T. Mitchell, Ph.D., C.T.S and George S. Everly, Jr. Ph.D., F.A.P.M., C.T.S. "Trauma – Any event outside the usual realm of human experience that is markedly distressing (e.g., evokes reactions of intense fear, helplessness, horror, etc.) Such traumatic stressors usually involve the perceived threat to one's physical integrity or to the physical integrity of someone in close proximity." (10) After the trauma, comes post-traumatic stress. Post-traumatic stress is defined as, "Very intense arousal subsequent to a traumatic stressor (trauma). Traumatic stress overwhelms coping mechanisms leaving individuals out of control and feeling helpless." (11)

If a person experiencing post-traumatic stress is not treated they may develop what has come to be known as post-traumatic stress disorder, or PTSD. PTSD is defined as follows. "The term applied as the official diagnosis of a post-traumatic stress syndrome which is characterized by symptoms of:

a. excessive excitability and arousal,
b. numbing withdrawal, and avoidance, and
c. repetitive, intrusive memories or recollections of the trauma and/or events related to the trauma,
d. duration of at least 1 month" (12)

Law enforcement officers are very well trained to see, and handle things that the general public would be horrified at. They have been trained to not show a lot of emotion, or fear. In fact they will try to disassociate from their emotions, so they will be better able to deal with a scene. We often call this disassociation going on "automatic pilot". It's as if they throw an internal switch that shuts off their emotions. The officer has a job to do, no matter how horrific the event their duty is to carry out that job. They don't have time to think about how terrible and tragic the scene is until after their job is done. If they could not manage their own emotions, they would have an extremely difficult time controlling, and working a crime scene. They will often not allow themselves to consider the awful, ghastly scene until hours or sometimes days or even months later. They may even consciously forget the scene altogether, but their subconscious will continue to try to process through what they have seen, smelled and heard.

Sometimes, by the time an officer finally realizes something is wrong the damage may have already begun. If they don't get the proper support they need, and they continue to suppress their emotions, they may get "stuck". Those who develop PTSD may suffer for months or even years before they get properly diagnosed. Because of the on- going "Global War on Terrorism" (or GWOT), there has been significant advances in diagnosing and treatment of PTSD. Where it used to take a minimum of six months for a diagnosis of PTSD, the symptoms can now be accurately diagnosed after 30 days of symptoms. The American Family Physicians records, "Before a diagnosis of PTSD can be made, symptoms must last for at least one month and must significantly disrupt normal activities." (13) PTSD can be the result of one major event, such as an officer involved shooting. It may also be the result of an accumulation effect from several events over time.

Not everyone will develop symptoms of PTSD after a traumatic event. Many people never develop symptoms. A person who has a good support system will be less likely to be effected by traumatic incidents. A good support system includes friendships outside of the department, family support, and often includes a Church or a relationship with a trusted chaplain. Some officers will get symptoms. Of those, some will have severe enough symptom to need to get help.

PTSD is not just a mental illness. It affects the physical, emotional, and sensual, parts of a person, as well as being a psychological disorder. The symptoms of PTSD run the gamut of the entire triune person. Many of these symptoms overlap in two or more of the three areas that make up who we are. These include the "pneuma" or spirit (character, ethics and morals), "psyche" or soul (mind, will and emotions) and the "soma" (physical body). Here are some of the common symptoms broken out by categories:

Symptoms affecting the Spirit:
1. Extreme Paranoia
2. Loss of Faith in God
3. Addictions to alcohol, drugs, sex (including affairs, prostitution, and pornography; especially where there wasn't a history of such behavior).
4. Poor work performance, and absenteeism – low work ethic
5. Increased cynicism

Symptoms affecting the Soul:
1. Extreme nightmares
2. Flashbacks of traumatic events
3. Sense of impending doom
4. Avoidance – Isolation, especially from family
5. Loss of interest in sex
6. Depression
7. Avoiding certain activities or areas that remind them of an event
8. Diminished interest in activities they used to enjoy
9. Sleeping too much, or sleeping much less than normal
10. Poor hygiene and weight management
11. Hard time remembering things, or thinking
12. Excessive irritability
13. Easily becoming angry
14. Obsessive/compulsive type behavior
15. Hyperactivity

Physical Symptoms:

1. Headaches
2. Chest pains
3. Muscle aches, especially upper back and neck
4. Frequent urination
5. Intestinal pains, irritable bowel syndrome (I.B.S.)
6. Excessive need for and use of antacids
7. Ulcers

Be aware, some of these symptoms are normal for a law enforcement officer. Some of the symptoms are common without being signs of psychological problems. PTSD is not something easy to identify, or to treat. If a person is suffering from PTSD, however, these symptoms will only continue to get worse over time if left untreated. PTSD is not something that normally just goes away by itself. It will continue to eat away at the person. Some of the symptoms may come and go, while others may be triggered by an outside stimulus, e.g. a flashback caused by a certain smell, a sound, or something the person sees.

My own personal experience as a Chaplain with PTSD can be traced back to Hurricane Katrina. The New Orleans Police Dept requested chaplain assistance, and I was deployed a few days after the devastating hurricane. You will recall, on top of the hurricane, there were levee breaks that flooded the city. The water was said to have risen nine feet in thirty minutes. I was sent to work with the law enforcement officers in New Orleans. I spent ten days on the ground, along with a small handful of other law enforcement chaplains from several different states.

Hurricane Katrina cost hundreds, if not thousands of lives. The devastation was everywhere, along with the suffocating heat and smell of rotten meat and garbage. On top of that, there was the very real danger from looters, and snipers; not to mention the danger from chemicals and disease in the water, and the possibility of poisonous snakes. We were also on the ground when Hurricane Rita came through a few days later.

When my deployment was over I was taken to the airport in Baton Rouge. There were no flights going in our out of New Orleans because of the destruction. It was about 16 hours before I could catch my flight towards home. I caught a few hours of restless sleep over night waiting for my flight. When I finally got home in California, it was a hot summer day. I remember getting in the car and enjoying the luxury of the air conditioning. We pulled into the driveway at our home. Thoughts of home were filling my mind when I stepped out of the car. There was a garbage can next to our house. As soon as I got out of the car, I was hit with the stench of rotting meat coming from the trash. My mind was immediately back in New Orleans, as all my muscles tensed, and my body was flooded with adrenaline.

Years after responding to the Hurricane Katrina ravaged area, when I smell rotting meat, my mind still immediately goes back there. I wasn't diagnosed with PTSD until three years after being deployed to New Orleans. There was always something in the back of my mind. I would tune out news programs about the area, and avoid pictures and stories of Katrina. Three years after being deployed there, I went back through New Orleans on business, and had a bad reaction, including sleeplessness, depression, a total lack of appetite and flashbacks.

I ended up with a serious illness after returning from New Orleans. After a couple of weeks I made an appointment with my doctor's office. My regular physician was not in, so I seen one of the other doctors at the office. When he walked in to my room, he said, "Don't I know you? You were in New Orleans right after Hurricane Katrina. I was volunteering there as well. How have you been since then?"

The doctor asking how I had been since being in New Orleans opened the door for me to talk about my symptoms of sleeplessness, depression, etc. I went in for what turned out to be a nasty lung infection, and got a referral to see a counselor about my depression and PTSD. I saw a counselor for about a year. She helped me tremendously.

PTSD and other stress related illnesses are probably some of the leading causes of early retirement, or resignations for law enforcement officers, and a major contributor to suicide.

I recall the story of a young man in Bible College who was enthusiastic about life; and full of optimism. He decided to list out all the good things in his life. He began his list with such things as his car, and girlfriend. He put down his looks, and intelligence, along with his talents and abilities. The list went on and on. He was so happy with his list that he decided to share his grand work with one of his favorite professors. The professor looked over his list, but rather than being impressed, he had a look of concern and disappointment on his face.

His professor looked at the young man and said, "This list is obviously well thought out, and must have taken a great deal of thought and meditation. However my young friend, there is one item missing from your list, without which, life is barely tolerable."

The young man took the list, glanced over it and said, "What could possibly be missing? My life is great, and I would be content to having nothing else added."

The wiser older professor looked at the young man with compassion in his eyes, and said, "Young man, many people have beauty, talent, wealth, power and even fame, but never find happiness. You can take your list, and put a big X through the whole thing. God reserves one thing for those fortunate few that He chooses as His own. Many people look for, and wait their entire lives, seeking out this one thing. The one thing you need to have a meaningful life that is not on your list is peace of mind."

The peace of mind that many officers seek can only be gotten at a price. Sometimes a law enforcement officer must have the courage to face and cope with the conflicts that affect them, and that disturb their peace. Sometimes it takes more courage for an officer to ask for help than to face down an armed, drugged up outlaw biker gang member. Often a trusted Chaplain is the first line of defense for the officer. The Chaplain may be the only person the officer trusts enough to be vulnerable and share their deepest concerns. You owe this officer as a Chaplain to be ready to handle this huge responsibility and trust.

Chaplains also need to be aware of their own self care. The Chaplain working alongside these officers may acquire PTSD themselves.   More common than PTSD among chaplains is something called Compassion Fatigue. Care-givers such as the Chaplain are very vulnerable to getting Compassion Fatigue. Compassion Fatigue is also known as Secondary Traumatic Stress Disorder, or Secondary Victimization. This comes from experiencing second hand the traumatic experiences of people involved in trauma work such as first responders, emergency room nurses, and chaplains. It is marked by a deep physical, emotional and spiritual exhaustion, and is often accompanied by deep emotional pain. The symptoms are very similar to PTSD.

Compassion Fatigue is generally caused by exposure to working with those in crisis, and grief. The typical person vulnerable to this may be a family member of someone who is grieving, or works with those in grief care. Often they are so busy-- they neglect to take care of themselves.

Chaplains have more of a susceptibility to Compassion Fatigue because they are often seen (and see themselves) as invulnerable. After all, "they have God to lean on".

Chaplains see and hear much of what a law enforcement officer experiences. They are sought out as the strong person who can handle hearing whatever you need to talk about. They also see more dead bodies, including children, in a year than the average officer will see in a career.

Law enforcement officers are also susceptible to Compassion Fatigue as they will often work lots of overtime contributing to feelings of exhaustion. This also holds true to the Chaplain who may be frequently called out in the middle of the night, disrupting their sleep. Physical exhaustion is often a pre-condition of Compassion Fatigue. As they are exposed to traumatic events, including second hand stories of traumatic events when already exhausted physically, they may begin experiencing symptoms.

Sleep deprivation not only contributes to Compassion Fatigue, but Compassion Fatigue can cause insomnia. This can create a vicious circle. A person with Compassion Fatigue will have trouble sleeping. Our brains process the traumas, and difficult experiences we have had during the day during times of deep sleep. Insomnia will prevent us from getting that deep sleep.

Aside from time off, there are other things to do to overcome Compassion Fatigue. First, acknowledge there is a problem. Take the time to care for yourself, and accept help. There is a need to re-establish emotional resilience. This is done by doing self care. This can include improving your diet, exercise, getting enough sunshine, and spending time with people you love. Most Chaplains and LEOs have a deep sense of duty, and do not like to take vacations. You need this downtime to refresh, renew, and to continue being good at the career you love so much.

The next step involves self examination. You need to really get to know yourself again, and come face to face with fear, anger, and maybe even self esteem issues. This is best done with the help of a good counselor, a pastor, fellow Chaplain, or a close friend/peer support who is a good listener, and is acquainted with Compassion Fatigue.

There are some things you can do to prevent Compassion Fatigue:

1.   One is to have quiet time every day. I spend mine in prayer, meditation and scripture reading.

2.   A second that is related, is to take time daily to "recharge the batteries". This may involve exercise, taking a walk, and/or taking the time to eat while doing nothing else. Break the habit of eating on the run.

3.   And three is to connect with people. Take the time everyday to have at least one meaningful conversation with a friend. Spending time with family or a close friend can work wonders in our lives. Holding the hand of someone you love has been proven to lower stress levels.

Unfortunately, time with friends and family is usually the first thing to go when we get too busy and too stressed.

We need to realize that we are vulnerable to the affects of being around too much grief. This second hand grief can wrap around our shoulders like a heavy wet sweater. Try as we may, we can't always throw this wrap off of our shoulders. There may be times when you try to remove this heavy garment of Compassion Fatigue until your arms become too exhausted to try anymore. We need to know when we have had too much, and get help for ourselves.

CHAPTER 7
DIVORCE – BROKEN PROMISES

The divorce rate among law enforcement officers is very high. Surveys among officers continue to reflect estimates of 75% of first marriages ending in divorce. There are many reasons specific to their career choice that can be pointed to as contributing factors to the high divorce rate. Many spouses of law enforcement officers never get used to shift work, the hours they have to spend alone, and the "non-existent holidays".

Another contributor to the divorce rate is a change in how the officer/spouse shows emotion. There is often an emotional distance experienced as the officer has to learn to control his or her emotions. This is often critical to their survival when responding to emergency situations. They have to learn to shut down their emotions on scenes. Unfortunately, they often have a hard time turning their emotions back on when they get off duty.

A young male officer sees himself as a hero when he is on the job, but it is hard to see yourself as a hero when you are told by your spouse to take out the garbage. The officer on the job has to solve difficult problems all day long, and if he or she expends all of their energy during the day, they may have little left for their family.

Generally speaking, there are seven different reasons that couples in America end up in divorce. Sometimes there is one primary reason, other times there may be a combination of the seven.   There are other factors that come into play with a law enforcement couple heightening the effects of these seven primary causes.

The first, and unfortunately the most common reason for divorce is sexual infidelity, or unfaithfulness. Adultery is the most devastating and disruptive force in a family, and is the most universally recognized and accepted reason for divorce. "It has been estimated that infidelity takes place in at least 70 percent of all marriages, although most unfaithfulness is brief and sometimes a one-time-only, spur of the moment occurrence. Even when the infidelity is confessed and discussed with one's mate, the marriage is likely to be affected." (14)   Unfaithfulness, even one occurrence, can destroy the strongest marriage bond.

Law enforcement officers tend to be adrenaline junkies. They will often seek the thrill and excitement from doing dangerous sports.   Unfortunately, they may also find themselves taking risks and looking for the thrill that can be had in an extramarital affair.

There are also many studies suggesting that people may become addicted to pornography because of events that happen to them.   These are often critical incidents that they have not dealt with in a healthy way, etc. The current relative ease and "Privacy" of online porn compounds this issue.

The second major cause of divorce is desertion. Desertion is mentioned as a common, accepted reason for divorce as far back as the New Testament.   In Christian circles, many people believe and teach that adultery is the only valid reason for divorce. However, Paul in his writings also taught that if an unbelieving spouse departs, let them depart. The Greek word used here as depart, can also be translated as desertion. If the spouse that has deserted their partner is gone, there really is no useful purpose in refusing to acknowledge the dissolution of the marriage.

Escalating incompatibility is the next cause of divorce. Many couples point to these incompatibilities or irreconcilable differences as their reason for divorce. Many people simply seem to drift apart, or may not have ever had that much in common to begin with. This seems to be a growing trend in divorces today. In law enforcement circles, when one spouse is a cop, and the other is not, the differences can often be magnified. The officer may think, and correctly so, that their spouse doesn't understand what they go through. Statistics seem to show there is a lower incidence of divorce among law enforcement couples when both partners are officers. There tends to be more compatibility, and understanding in their relationships, since they both see and experience the same kinds of things.

The social sanctions that once made divorce something only whispered about, have for the most part been done away with. Divorce is now very common, and socially much more acceptable than it once was.

Social attitudes in our society have changed both in regards to marriage and divorce; as well as to the precedence of people's careers to the exclusion of everything else. "Some people maintain the view that self-realization, career advancement, and personal fulfillment are such major goals in life that everything else – including a commitment to marriage – must take second place." (15) This philosophy and the fact that divorce has lost much of its social stigma makes divorce for reasons of incompatibility more widely accepted today.

The fifth major cause of divorce comes from an immature attitude in one or both partners. This would include such things as an inability to keep commitments, insensitivity to the needs of their spouse, a tendency to try and dominate the other partner, and a generally self centered attitude. These kinds of attitudes spur on arguments and hard feelings. They make it difficult to work through the rough patches in a marriage. A good marriage takes a lot of work. There needs to be a level of maturity in both partners. Many people never seem able to develop this maturity.

The sixth major cause of divorce, which is very common in law enforcement officers, is persistent stress. Stress is a big part of the average officer's job, and much of this comes home to his or her family. Persistent stress can put a lot of pressure on any marriage. When an officer is facing a lot of stress on the job, they will cram their emotions, and not communicate as well with their spouse. They may think they are protecting their spouse by not talking about what is going on with their job, but instead of feeling protected, the spouse may feel left out and ignored. This leads to a vicious circle of more stress for the officer: strained relations at home leads to more stress on the job, which causes more stress at home, and so on and so on. (16)

The last of the seven major causes of divorce, is less prevalent than the other six, but is still common enough to be included in this list. The last cause is physical, mental, and/or spiritual abuse. A civilian would likely think that spousal abuse and domestic violence would be rare in law enforcement marriages. The assumption is cops are held to a higher standard than most of society, so there would be no abuse. Unfortunately, this is not the case. "A relatively large percentage of law enforcement officers may be involved in domestic violence, to some extent because of the nature of their work and the organizational stresses they face." (17) Spousal abuse among law enforcement families can be more dangerous, because of the training that the officer receives, and the ready access to a firearm. If the abused person happens to be the officer, the abuser may try to force the officer/spouse to pull out their weapon.

An officer is trained to be in control at all times; his or her body is a weapon; and they have quick access to lethal force. When you mix all of these ingredients together, and add in stress - sometimes an abuser falls out of the mix.

A note to the Chaplain: As a Christian, I never like the idea of divorce, and would prefer, and will push for reconciliation whenever possible. One clear exception to the Biblical stance against divorce is unfaithfulness of one spouse towards another. By committing domestic violence against their spouse, the offending spouse, male or female (women are sometimes the abuser), has broken their wedding vow. They have proven themselves unfaithful to the promises they made on their wedding day. I would never recommend a person stay in an abusive relationship. Furthermore, people who condone telling a person to stay in a relationship where they are being abused; or worse yet condemn them for trying to get out of an abusive relationship on "Biblical grounds" are on very shaky ground theologically.

Divorce is an ugly word, which unfortunately is very common among law enforcement officers. Let's re-visit the three parts of a person, i.e. the body, soul and spirit. There are three levels of intimacy within a marriage. Here is an illustration of what happens "when boy meets girl." When a guy first meets a woman, he may say "Hey, she looks GOOOOD! And her perfume smells really nice." This is the physical level using the senses. He may next think, "I think I would like to get to know her better." And later, "I think I am falling in love with her." This is the level of the soul, or the psyche where our mind, will, and emotions lie. Unfortunately, many relationships never make it beyond the physical and emotional levels. The spirit level is where, again, we have our character, our morality and ethics. Our spirit is where we make a commitment to stick with a marriage, and we become as one with our spouse. Physical lust may not last (everybody gets old), and feelings of love are fickle. The commitment to make a marriage work, takes a lot of effort. It takes work to keep the romance and excitement alive, and not give up when things get tough. Marriages often fail without the spirit to keep two people striving to stay together as a couple. These are principles that are talked about more in sections three and four.

CHAPTER 8
SUICIDE – THE END OF A LEGACY

There was a survey conducted in 1997 at the COPS (Concerns of Police Survivors) seminar of 500 law enforcement officers from nine major cities in the United States. The purpose of the survey was to determine if officers would ever consider suicide as an option and why. The results of the survey were shocking. A full 98% of those surveyed said they would consider suicide under certain circumstances. Here is the list of circumstances cited in this survey:

- Death of a child or spouse
- Loss of a child or spouse through divorce
- Terminal illness
- Responsibility for partner's death
- Killed someone out of anger
- Indictment
- Feeling alone
- Sexual accusations
- Loss of job due to a conviction of a crime
- Being locked-up (18)

Suicide in the United States runs at about an average of 16 for every 100,000 people a year. It is presumed by most experts to be much higher among law enforcement officers. It has been estimated that a law enforcement officer is eight times more likely to die of suicide than at the hand of a perpetrator. The suicide rate among LEO's has not been widely studied, and it is often difficult to get accurate information because of the stigma related to suicide in the United States.

A number of factors may lead a person to think their only way out is to take their own life. "Possible reasons for the high suicide rate include: continuous exposure to human misery, overbearing police bureaucracy, shift work, social strain, marital difficulties, and inconsistencies of the criminal justice system, alcohol abuse and lack of control over working conditions." (19)   The suicide rates for those who are alcoholics is about 270 for every 100,000 compared to 16 for every 100,000 in the general public. The problem with alcohol is that it at first does relieve tension, but it also is a depressant, and in the long run makes depression worse.   Depression is another major factor in people who take their own lives. The rate for those in the general public who are suffering from depression is around 230 for every 100,000.

The most common profile for a person who will attempt and complete a suicide is a white male 45 years or older. They are divorced or alone, and normally have a drinking or drug problem. Alcoholics that are off of alcohol within their first year of sobriety are at the greatest risk. Being sober is a major change to their lifestyle. They are often unemployed, or in a dead-end job.

One of the primary personality traits developed in a cadet during academy, and later as a street cop is to always be in control. They are taught to be in control of the scene, be in control of those around the scene, and be in control of themselves. This is an officer safety issue and is vitally important in doing their job. Whenever an officer is having a difficult time keeping charge of a scene or incident, they are taught to take control. They use an escalating scale of force to bring a situation under control. If control cannot be gained by any other means, they are taught to use lethal force to take out the problem that is keeping them from taking control, such as a person with a gun that is trying to kill them. This kind of power and responsibility to control can be very stressful. We also know from the previous section how the work the officer is engaged in leads them down a path to cynicism. So following this line of logic, we have a person who has been trained to maintain control no matter what up to and including the use of lethal force, who is stressed out and cynical.

When an officer comes to a point in their lives where they feel like they don't have power over their own situation, the results can be devastating. It may lead to a suicide attempt. It is not unusual for an officer to commit suicide after a significant change in their lives surrounding a loss. This could be a retirement, a divorce, or the loss of a loved one. A common way they choose to deal with the feeling of a loss of control is to put the barrel of their gun in their mouths and pull the trigger. Many of them say they may not be able to control anything else, but they can control how and when they will take their own life.

The pain of hopelessness is the biggest contributor to suicide. A person comes to the point where they feel like they can't control their own behavior, feelings, or circumstances. This feeling of despair is not usually something that comes on all at once, but typically it comes on slowly over time and grows until it is perceived as being insurmountable. It has been described as standing in a huge forest where you can't see any of the trees because you have one tree that is right in your face all the time. No matter which way you turn your head, all you can see is bark. Their entire focus is on suicide – the only way out for them. No matter how they try, they can't seem to break free of this.

The squad room of a police department historically has not been a place that is open to discussing feelings and emotions. It has been described as a den of wild dogs that attack any sign of weakness. Only the strong will be allowed to survive. The officer who is feeling overwhelmed and depressed will often not talk to his or her partner, or other co-workers. They are used to keeping up the appearance of being in charge and stoic. It is no better when they go home. They are so accustomed to turning off their emotions and not sharing what is going on at work, they don't share with their spouse either. They may feel they have nowhere to turn for help. Even if they know their resources, they often would rather "eat their own gun" than admit their weakness or that they need help. They can't tolerate the stigma that may be associated with seeking out mental health support, or the appearance of being weak.

It is less common for female officers to complete suicide than their male counterparts. Statistics show fewer women in the general population complete suicide than do men. Though some recent studies suggest this may be a changing trend. Women, including female officers, tend to be more open with their emotions and stress, and are willing to reach out and ask for help. Female officers tend to avoid competitiveness. They are more proactive in making a conscious effort to take positive steps to reduce their stress. They are more likely to do such things as taking time off from work, spending time with family, and finding positive stress reducers.

The progression from the young altruistic recruit in academy, who is ready to save the world, to the officer on their knees with a gun in their mouth ready to end their misery, is too common. It has been described by Cindy Goss, a certified counselor for drug and alcohol abuse, working in New York for Erie County. She says, "Graduate frequently exposed to blood, gore and danger. Does not unburden these horrors on spouse. Spouse wouldn't understand. A few drinks with the guys after work helps to unwind. Fellow cops understand. Can't trust civilians. Can't admit troubles even to fellow cops; would be considered a wimp. Can't trust fellow cops. Drinking increases. Spouse takes off. Gun is handy." (20)

In the next section we will talk more about peer support and chaplains who are trained to recognize suicidal tendencies, and how to intervene with the officer.

SECTION III
CHARACTER RE-ENFORCED

Chaplain Terry Morgan

CHAPTER 9
SHARPENING THE SWORD

Proverbs 27:17, "*As iron sharpens iron, so one man sharpens another.*"(1)

The previous two sections of this book draw a pretty gloomy picture for our law enforcement officers. They show the stark reality of what police work is really like and the cold hard facts of the effects of law enforcement work on the officer from academy through retirement. There is good news however. There are people specially called by God and trained to come alongside of the officers: to be their moral compass: and to help them to resist the cynicism that claims so many of them. The work of Chaplains, peer support, and psychological counseling is becoming more widely accepted in law enforcement circles. There is a trend towards having more healthy officers and law enforcement families.

Jesus Christ was a master storyteller. He often taught lessons using a tool called a parable. A parable is a story with a moral message within the narrative. One of the best ways to get a point across, is to "paint a word picture" with a story. I often use stories to illustrate a point, or capture the attention of a person reading an article. It serves to entice them to read the rest of the story. This section starts out with an amusing little story, which helps to illustrate the role of a Chaplain.

There once was a little parakeet named Rocky. Rocky was a carefree, happy little bird, always chirping and singing. But then one day, everything changed. Poor Rocky, he never saw it coming. One second he was in his house, sitting peacefully up on his perch and the very next second he was **sucked in, washed up and totally blown away.**

The trouble began when Rocky's owner, Dave, decided to clean Rocky's cage. Dave thought the easiest way to clean it would be with the vacuum cleaner. He took off the attachment and stuck the vacuum cleaner hose in the bottom of Rocky's cage. The cell phone rang, and Dave turned to pick it up. He was barely able to say hello when he heard the awful sound. Schwoomp! Rocky got sucked in by the vacuum cleaner!

Dave immediately realized what happened, dropped his cell phone, and turned off the vacuum cleaner. He ripped open the vacuum cleaner and tore apart the bag. He found Rocky dazed but alive. Rocky was covered with dirt and soot, so his owner grabbed him and ran for the bathroom. Dave turned on the faucet full blast, and frantically shoved Rocky under the gushing torrent of water.

Most of the dirt and soot came off, but now Rocky was soaking wet and shivering. Dave did what any compassionate bird lover would do. He grabbed the blow dryer, set it for its highest setting, and blasted Rocky with hot air. Poor Rocky never knew what hit him.

A few days later, someone asked Dave how his little parakeet was doing after his critical incident. Dave told them, "Well he doesn't sing anymore; mostly all he does is sit on his perch with a blank look on his face staring straight ahead".

Most crisis situations arise suddenly and unexpectedly. The Chaplain is often called upon to bring comfort, hope, and peace in the midst of chaos.

We have learned Chaplains must also take care of themselves. As we respond to the many needs of law enforcement, we may take it for granted that we see the worst that life has to offer on a regular basis. It's easy for us to fall into the trap of thinking "We have God, so we don't need anything else." Don't be deceived! Compassion Fatigue can take out the best of us (see chapter 6 for more information on Compassion Fatigue).

There is one more story I would like to share to further clarify the role of the Law Enforcement Chaplain. The Bible tells about a time Paul was on a ship bound for Italy. A mighty storm came up and completely blew their ship off course. A huge wind with the force of a hurricane called the "Northeaster" hit them all at once. Not only were they fighting for their lives against this incredible storm, but they were also totally blown off course. They were lost at sea, not knowing where they were.

The sailors did all they could to save themselves, and the ship. They threw all of the cargo overboard trying to lighten the ship. They trimmed their sails, and finally on the third day they even threw the ships tackle overboard. Nothing they did was helping. The fierce wind and rain threatened to tear their ship apart and cast them all into the sea, where the huge waves would surely drown every one of them.

The Bible describes the despair the sailors and passengers felt in Acts 27: 20. It says: "When neither sun nor stars appeared for many days and the storm continued raging, we finally gave up all hope of being saved." (2) All of them had given up any hope of survival. That night, something miraculous occurred. God sent his messenger, an angel, to Paul and told him God would save him and everyone on the ship. Paul told everyone what had happened and encouraged them to have faith and hang on a little longer. They were given a new sense of hope, and found the strength to keep going. In the end, they lost the ship, but they all survived. Not one of them was lost to the angry, stormy sea.

Traumatic experiences happen to all of us at one time or another. Some are worse than others, and sometimes, they hit a person so hard and unexpectedly, that they **suck them in, wash them up, and totally blow them away**. As a Chaplain, you are called to intervene. You will be in a position to bring peace and calm to a situation. You will be able to make a difference in the lives you touch, both law enforcement and civilian. I would like to challenge you to go into your community as the messenger from God, and bring God's peace, and hope to people in the midst of the darkest storms of their lives.

The Chaplain is called by God to come along side the officer. As one piece of iron can be used to sharpen another, so the presence of the Chaplain can help to develop and mold the character of the officer. Chaplains can stimulate the mind and spirit of the officer, and be there to counsel and guide through critical incidents, and other issues of life. The chaplain is often considered the "moral compass" for the officer, always pointing true North. The chaplain challenges them to maintain their course and not drift, but to live their life, and work their career with a high moral and ethical standard.

Just as not everyone will be able to become a law enforcement officer, not everyone that expresses an interest in being a law enforcement Chaplain will necessarily be a good fit for the position. The Chaplain should be a Chaplain by calling, not simply by choice. It is clearly not a job that just anybody can do. There is a lot expected of a law enforcement Chaplain; probably more than is fair to ask or that most people are willing to tolerate. It has been my experience that the best law enforcement chaplains are those who have served in a crisis, or chaplain role in the community. They have a good understanding of grief. They have experience working with people in crisis. This person may or may not be an experienced minister, or pastor of a congregation (though that experience can be very helpful). Although there is great benefit in having a pastoral background, this doesn't seem to be the biggest deciding issue in who will make a good law enforcement chaplain.

In the next chapter, many of the requirements and expectations of the Chaplain will be laid out and expounded upon.

CHAPTER 10
RAISING THE SHIELD

The Chaplain position in a law enforcement agency is a spiritual service position. For this reason, it is imperative that the Chaplain be a person of faith. Being a person of faith, they will be able to recognize the calling of God to the ministry of being a Chaplain. A criminal history background check will be a necessary screening tool, since the Chaplain will be working very closely with officers, and potentially very sensitive situations. There are many requirements and expectations of a law enforcement Chaplain. This chapter will address these requirements and expectations.

It takes time for new Chaplains to establish their role, and earn the trust of the beat cops. Just because you have the title, doesn't mean you automatically will be trusted, or accepted by the line officer. Officers will look hard at any new Chaplain. They will be watching to see if your actions and attitude reflect your faith. This doesn't mean the Chaplain should go around quoting scripture, and preaching to the officers. Chaplains need to live their lives in such a way that their faith is easy, gentle, caring and trustworthy.

The first section of this book discusses the reality of the high levels of stress experienced by those in law enforcement. The Chaplain also must have a high tolerance for stress, and endurance to work long hours. The average Chaplain will see more dead children, suicide victims, death and destruction in a year, than the average officer will see in their entire career. Remember that those are the kinds of critical incidents that the Chaplain will most likely be called to. These kinds of calls will have an effect on you, and will change you, just as they do cops that go to the same kinds of scenes. You probably won't see the same officers on every critical incident unless the department is very small.

It's important to know your own limits as a Chaplain. You can't save everybody, or take on everyone's pain. When a cruise ship begins sinking in the middle of the ocean the crew will start lowering lifeboats into the water. Each lifeboat can comfortably hold a certain number of passengers, and is capable of holding a few more in an emergency. At some point however, if you keep loading people into one lifeboat, the lifeboat will sink, and be of no use to any of the passengers. In much the same way, you need to know the answer to the question, "How big is your lifeboat?" How much can you take on before you start to flounder and sink?

Sometimes you as a Chaplain have to take time out for yourself to rest, reflect, and recharge. You may suffer burnout from being purely exhausted. You may develop compassion fatigue from trying to take on too much of people's pain, heart ache, and agony of soul without any relief. "The counseling profession in general, because of the intense involvement in other people's problems required of therapists, can easily lead to burnout. Clinicians in police stress programs may be especially vulnerable to burnout because much of the counseling they do revolves around issues of injury and death and because staff typically work long hours, often at night and on weekends." (3)

Appearances are very important. If you drink alcohol, be aware that it leaves an odor that is not easily covered up by mouthwash, or breath mints. You may be called upon at any time, and if you happen to smell of alcohol it will definitely leave an impression. Other offending odors are tobacco, strong perfume or after-shave, bad breath or body odors.

Even in nature, we see how important appearance is. Allow me tell a story that illustrates this. It had been a long hard winter. The wolves were hungry, and had been having a hard time finding prey. This day however, they caught the scent of a moose. A moose is difficult to bring down. They would normally avoid them because they were so big and dangerous and could easily kill one of them with its antlers or hoofs. But, if they were successful, they would have full bellies.

The pack began surrounding the moose. Each one took their position. Soon, the alpha female began rushing the moose's head. She wouldn't get close enough to get hit by the hooves. She only wanted to scare it – to get it to panic and run. If they could panic the moose, and get it to run, they could bite its back legs, causing it to lose blood, and weaken.

The moose stood its ground. It angrily pawed the ground and snorted. The wolves kept up the lunging for a while to no avail. Unexpectedly, the wolves all left. They knew it was fruitless. This animal was too strong and too healthy. They wouldn't waste anymore of their precious strength on it. They knew if they couldn't get the moose to panic in the first few minutes, they would never be able to conquer it. They would continue their hunt for a weaker or more inexperienced animal. Their first perception was that they could take the beast, but now they knew they were wrong.

There is an old saying, "perception is reality". In other words, your image or how people see you will influence what they think about you. What image are you projecting? Are you projecting professionalism, and confidence? Or are you wearing a wrinkled shirt, with unkempt hair, projecting an "I don't care" attitude?

An officer once told me that he always makes sure his shoes are clean, his uniform pressed, and his hair is neat and clean. His attitude is he wants to give the appearance of being a professional. He also said the cop who allows his shoes to be scuffed up, and wears a wrinkled uniform has a public perception of being untrained and unprofessional. He then asked me, "If you were a criminal out to kill a cop, which one would you be more likely to attack? The cop who appeared trained and ready or the one who looked unprepared, and untrained?" The answer is obvious.

We all make judgments about people several hundred times a day. It is something we don't even think about. It's a subconscious transfer of information, and is usually done in an instant. It is based upon our culture, our value system, and our own expectations. They can be positive or negative.

How we perceive a person's image is important. It has been described as a kind of shorthand for understanding what is going on around us. If we had to make a conscious decision about what was happening in every situation, we would be constantly under information overload. So we use this as a coping mechanism – a way to deal with the world around us.

Fair or unfair, people do "judge a book by its cover". We make these kinds of split second judgments every day. For example, a person is more likely to trust a doctor in their surgery, if the doctor dresses in sensible clothing and behaves in a professional manner. The same person would likely not trust the doctor if the surgeon showed up for work in bizarre clothing, and intermittently sang children's songs.

To break it down, 55% of first impressions are based on our appearance. 38% are based on voice, how we speak, etc. While only 7% of first impressions are based on actual content. In other words, people believe what they see before what they hear. This is especially true in a crisis. They base their opinion mostly on how you look and what you are doing.

A good question for every chaplain (and every officer) is, "How do you want to be seen?" Most chaplains want to be perceived as being trustworthy; dependable; caring; and a safe person. I am not one to tell a person how to look, give my opinion about tattoos, or body piercings, etc. However, our physical appearance will have an effect on how people in our community react to and treat us. It does matter how the chaplain looks, smells, dresses, etc.

So, another question might be, "Why should we care about how other people see us?" In Verbal Judo training, we learn to talk to people in such a way as to leave a positive impression on them. Officers using these techniques will find they help make most calls go smoother, with fewer headaches, and fewer citizen complaints. A negative perception by our communities can negatively affect our jobs. It creates unnecessary concerns about law enforcement in general. It can create a false image of the whole department. This negative image creates more work for the officer.

Wolves on average will harass about a dozen moose before they find one they are able to excite into running away. It's only when they get them to run that they can begin the slow process of killing the moose by biting their legs, and causing them to bleed and weaken. Then eventually they will bite their necks and kill them. Maybe that old officer had a good point about criminals picking on the perceived weak, and untrained. Remember, perception is reality. Dress for success. Wear your chaplain uniform with pride, and the dignity it deserves.

O.K., enough about appearances. Let's talk about our titles. When you become a chaplain, "Chaplain" becomes your title. There are no Lutheran Chaplains, or Pentecostal Chaplains, or Roman Catholic Chaplains; there are just Chaplains. If you keep your denominational title, you will limit yourself to only those officers that attend churches of your denomination. This also goes for political and religious titles. There are not Republican Chaplains, Democrat Chaplains – Father Chaplains, or Pastor Chaplains. There are just Chaplains. The more you limit yourself with titles, the less effective you will be. The Apostle Paul said, "Though I am free and belong to no man, I make myself a slave to everyone, to win as many as possible." (4) And again, "To the weak I became weak, to win the weak. I have become all things to all men so that by all possible means I might save some." (5)

Another qualification for being a Chaplain is integrity. Members of a law enforcement agency or department need to be able to count on the integrity, and ethical behavior of the Chaplain. The credibility of the Chaplain will be compromised if they are caught in any un-ethical practice. This means the Chaplain obeys all laws. The Chaplain should never put an officer in a position where they are uncomfortable, or tempted to compromise because of our role or title. For example, if the Chaplain is pulled over for breaking a traffic law, they should never use their position or department ID badge to try to get out of the ticket.

The Chaplain needs to be above reproach in action and words. The use of profanity, crude speech, or joking can lead to problems. There was an incident when I witnessed a male chaplain make a sexually suggestive joke to a female friend of his. He said in a suggestive tone something like, "hey little girl, do you want a cookie?" This kind of behavior is totally unacceptable for a Chaplain and should never be tolerated. Not only is this kind of behavior sending a very inappropriate message, it could even end up in a lawsuit for sexual harassment.

The Chaplain should have a genuine interest in law enforcement officers. They should demonstrate this interest through spending time at the station, going to briefings and on ride alongs. The Chaplain needs to have a desire to work with law enforcement officers without showing overly undue admiration, nor at the other extreme, with a wish to "reform" the police officer's world. They need to show a desire to get to know the officers as people, including their families, attending special events like graduations, etc. They need to learn all they can about law enforcement, so they can be a benefit rather than a hindrance to the officer on ride-alongs. This doesn't mean the Chaplain should ever consider themselves cops, or try to be like the officers around them. To win the respect and admiration of the officers, you need to, "Prove that you have something beneficial to offer and will maintain confidentiality – and then rely on word of mouth."(6) The officer expects the Chaplain to be different, and will usually "place them on a pedestal." Accept the fact that they treat you as something special, and don't try to be "just one of the guys".

Law enforcement Chaplains, and Chaplaincy programs in general may not be utilized in an agency. If the officers do not believe the Chaplain genuinely cares about, and is interested in them, they will be reluctant to use their services. There may be a passive type of acceptance or tolerance until the Chaplain is able to get beyond the "blue wall". This takes time, visibility, patience, and a lot of effort.

The attitude of the Chaplain should be one of strength, yet gentleness. The Chaplain needs to show "enough assertiveness to counter the habit some law enforcement officers have of acting intimidating, but also a manner that is warm, caring, and empathic." (7) Most of the time, the Chaplain will be expected to suppress their own emotions, and allow those they are helping to show theirs. You are not there to express your grief, but to help the officer or citizens to work through theirs. If a Chaplain whines, complains, or is a faultfinder, they will find no tolerance among the officers in the department. If you are rude and impatient, or use foul language, you will quickly lose all credibility.

Most officers will watch their mouths and language around you, and may even apologize when curse words come out of their mouths. This shows respect for you, but also comes from a belief that clergy will judge them for their words or actions. Our goal as a Chaplain is to become a person, perhaps the only person in the officer's life that will never judge or condemn them for their words or actions. The goal of the Chaplain is to be totally accepted and trusted by the officer, so the officers can be themselves, open honest and safe. I can't emphasize enough the importance of never using foul language around an officer. It will always tarnish their view of the

Chaplain. At the same time, don't make them feel guilty if they choose to use profanity.

When the Chaplain is called to a scene they are expected to arrive as quickly as they legally can. They then should most often be the last to leave. It is important to take the time to really help. Many clergy have the awful habit of breezing through a home where a death has occurred; saying a quick prayer, and heading out the door. In most instances this is because they have not received any training or instruction in working with someone who has lost a loved one, and/or they are very uncomfortable with this role. This is not something normally taught in seminary. The Chaplain should have the training and be prepared to stay until their presence is no longer bringing comfort, or they are no longer needed.

It has always been my habit to try to help clergy who are called to a traumatic scene by giving them a little guidance in working with families. Remember the general clergy will likely not be allowed to cross the crime scene tape, whereas the chaplain usually always will. When the clergy is allowed in, remember they are the clergy for the family, not you. I always defer to the clergy as the family's spiritual shepherd responsible for their spiritual welfare. Try to make them as comfortable as possible while giving the victims a warm hand off to them.

Another qualification for a Chaplain is being both a good listener, and affirmer. Building relationships is vital to the success of a Chaplain program. They will begin to gain the confidence of the officer, by showing they are truly interested in what the officer has to say. Most clergy are great talkers. Most of their work in the Church is preaching and teaching. However, few clergy have ever learned to be good listeners. The biggest part of our job as chaplains is to draw people out and get them to talk. Then, to listen to what they have to say.

It's important that we find something affirmative to say about the officer whenever we can. Cops are not often told they did a good job on a call or with dealing with a particularly difficult person. When going on a ride-along, you should always be looking for something that the officer does very well, and then praise them for it. This should not be artificial, or patronizing, but done with sincerity. If they did a good job, tell them. It will bring appreciation for the Chaplain and open many doors when you give them sincere praise for a job well done.

The Chaplain needs to be very honest. If you say you are going to do something, do it. If you can't do something, don't say you can or will. The Chaplain is always being watched to see if they are trustworthy, and what kind of integrity they have.

You may already have a degree from a reputable school, university, or seminary. However, most schools do not give you all of the tools you will need to be effective as a Chaplain. Even many psychiatrists and psychologists I have spoken to over the years, have never learned the specific types of things one needs to know to be effective as a Chaplain. (Appendix A has a few resources listed for further education.) Some of the classes that would be helpful to someone who is interested in becoming a Chaplain might read thusly:

1.   Introduction to Peer Support
2.   Listening Skills
3.   Critical   Incident   Stress   Debriefing   and Management
4.   Grief and bereavement
5.   Alcohol and Substance abuse
6.   Death notifications
7.   Cultural Diversity
8.   Stress management
9.   Officer involved shootings
10.   Officer injury/death in the line of duty
11.   Confidentiality
12.   Constitutional issues
13.   Crisis Counseling
14.   Crime scene integrity
15.   Suicide prevention/intervention/post-vention

Nothing can substitute for a good education. The more you know about law enforcement, crisis counseling, and the unique attributes of counseling law enforcement officers the more effective you will be as a Chaplain. This book is a good start, and gives a lot of guidelines and information, but it is not meant to be all-inclusive. One way to show you really care about the officers you serve is to continually get educated. There is constant research being done, and new information being developed. Don't get caught up in "the way we have always done it".

Finally let me reiterate one more time. The law enforcement officer will always look at the Chaplain as someone special. Don't try to fit in by being a "cop wannabe", or by using foul language or telling off-color jokes. You may thing you fit in by doing these kinds of things, but you will never have the credibility that you would have by holding to a higher standard. As a Chaplain, you need to accept that the officers will always look at you and treat you as someone special. After all, that is why you have been ordained. (8)

CHAPTER 11
SHINING THE ARMOUR

Availability is one of the keys to being effective in the ministry of a Chaplain. If you remain "cooped up" in an office somewhere all of the time, your services will very likely not be called upon. It is vital that the Chaplain be highly visible. This involves going to briefings, special events, and regularly doing ride-alongs. The more proactive and visible you are, the more likely you will be called upon when needed. In most agencies there is a constant flow of new officers. They may be transferring from another department, which may or may not utilize chaplains, or they may be fresh out of academy. Often times an officer will not use the services of a Chaplain because they forget they are available, or in some sad instances, they don't even realize the department has a Chaplain.

One very effective method of being visible, and touching the lives of officers, is what I like to call, "vending machine counseling". A great deal of Chaplain counseling "takes place spontaneously around the water cooler, over coffee…" (9) or wherever the officer and a Chaplain happen to meet. If the conversation becomes such that privacy is needed, the Chaplain can take the officer aside, or they can arrange a time to meet over coffee somewhere, or set a counseling appointment.

There was a talk show recently discussing the role of mental health workers and military Chaplains in the war in Iraq. The mental health workers and Chaplains were some of the first deployed, and stayed with the troops throughout the battles. Dr. Ritchie a psychiatrist for the medical corps., referring to the Chaplains and mental health workers, said they were there "both before the soldiers deployed and then in theater with them, working especially closely with them after any particularly traumatic event, and then they're also helping them get ready to return to the United States and, once they get back here, will also be available, working with the troops, to see if they are having difficulties and, if they are, to help treat them." (10) This is a good example of how the law enforcement Chaplains should be out there "in the trenches" working with the officers. There is a saying that rings true with law enforcement chaplain work. You have to be willing to pay your dues in order to be accepted. Being with the officers doing DUI checkpoints in the rain and cold; doing ride-alongs, and sit-alongs; going to briefings; attending graduations, retirement parties, weddings and funerals. Nothing can take the place of just spending time with and around the officers.

Be patient when trying to win the trust of law enforcement officers. Most of them have been trained, and have been learning since academy to trust no one. The director of the Metro-Dade Police Department's mental health services section talked about the time it takes for a new program to gain the trust of officers. They said, "It takes a minimum of three years for a program staff to win the confidence of officers, even if the staff are officers themselves." (11) The director for Erie County, New York's Law Enforcement Employee Assistance Program said, "It takes about one year to get a program up and running and several more years to generate widespread awareness and support." (12) It makes sense to take your time, and do a better job when starting a Chaplain program. Remember, not every officer is going to "love you" at first. Make your priority going to those officers that do like you, and want you around. Then allow them to promote the Chaplain program by word of mouth. It is counter-productive to try to influence, or win over officers that are unsupportive of, or downright opposed to the Chaplain program.

One of the fastest ways to get to know officers is by doing ride-alongs with them. There are a few things to do to prepare for a ride-along. The first thing to do is get permission from the sergeant. (This is assuming that you already have ride-along privileges from the Chief or Sheriff). Depending on how well you know those in the department, you can either ask the sergeant to assign you to someone, or ask for an officer to volunteer to take you. It has been my experience that if you ask the sergeant to assign you to an officer, often they will assign you to someone that really needs to talk, or that has been through a recent critical incident.

Before starting to do ride-alongs, you should have received training in fire-arms familiarity, crime-scene integrity, and some sort of self-defense to know when to duck, and where to seek cover if being shot at, etc. Be familiar with some of the basic call codes the department uses. The better trained you are before you go on a ride-along, the more comfortable you will feel, and the more at ease the officer will be with you.

Check to see that you have the right equipment before you ride. This would include a bullet proof vest (remember, when you are with the officer, you become a target); comfortable shoes that you could run in if you had to; and a warm jacket, even if it is warm outside (you may end up needing it before the end of the shift). You need to carry a small flashlight, at least one pair of rubber gloves, a pen and notebook, and a granola bar or other non-perishable type of snack, in case you are stuck out somewhere for several hours. I also suggest carrying a set of handcuffs, and a handcuff key. You should be able to fit all of this into a fanny pack.

Do not come to do the ride-along armed. You are riding as a Chaplain, not as a cop. In most departments the chaplain is considered "non-combat personnel." Be prepared to be a Pastor/Chaplain to the officer, and not another cop.

Be sure to go to the briefing before you go on your ride-along, and take notes. It is as important to be mentally prepared before your ride-along as it is to be physically prepared. You need to realize that something very serious could happen during the shift, and that the officer (or sometimes even the Chaplain) may have to use force against an individual.

Ask the officer you are riding with for his or her extra key to the patrol car before going to the car. When you get in the car, ask the officer how to release the shotgun; how to make a call out in case of an emergency; and about the proper use of any other equipment in the car. Don't assume that they will explain the equipment at some point during the ride-along, because they may in turn assume that you know how everything works. Most officers take pride in their patrol car, and are happy to explain all of the "gadgets" to you.

Ask the officer to let you know if they **don't** want you to get out of the car on some scenes. There may be certain scenes that may be very unsafe, such as a traffic stop on the freeway, when you shouldn't get out of the car. You should never be a distraction to the officer on a ride-along.

Pay attention to cross streets, and land marks. If something really bad happens, and the officer gets hurt and can't call for help, you may need to be the one to make that call. It is imperative that you know where you are at all times. Many patrol cars now have global tracking systems, which can be activated by simply pushing a button on the console, however, this should be done in addition to calling in for help.

You may be called with the officer to respond to a wide variety of incidents. The Chaplain should be an extra set of eyes, and watch the officer's back. You may be asked to keep an eye on other suspects to prevent them from destroying evidence, possible escape, or assaulting the officer. Don't be distracted by the actions of the officer, and don't converse with remaining suspects or bystanders.

116

If you see something dangerous, or a potential threat that the officer may have missed, speak out loud and get his or her attention. If you are watching a suspect, use an authoritative voice, and command the suspect to stay put. Say it loud enough for the officer to hear so they are aware of what is going on.

If you observe something that the officer may have missed, be sure and let them know. There have been several times I have found key pieces of evidence, such as a handgun that the officer missed simply by being observant. By being the extra set of eyes for an officer, they will appreciate your being an asset to them rather than a liability.

Know your surroundings when you are on a scene. Know where you can get too quickly for cover if the need arises. Try to not block the officer's view and never get between the officer and the suspect. Never stand in or block a doorway. Don't block high intensity lights, and don't distract the officer with constant movement. If it is nighttime, never use the spotlight backlighting the officer if he or she is outside of the car. Use common sense in most situations and you will be fine. Finally, follow any and all instructions you receive from the officer quickly.

One of the toughest types of calls is unusual during a ride-along, but may happen at any time. This is an "Officer needs assistance" call. This would be when an officer you are riding with gets in a situation, such as a fight, or is injured, and needs immediate help. With these kinds of calls, the Chaplain needs to immediately, but calmly radio dispatch saying, "Officer needs assistance". Identify yourself, and give your call sign and location. Don't try to use call codes, simply speak in plain English, and tell the dispatcher what is going on.

Quickly evaluate the situation. Determine how many suspects are involved, and what kind of confrontation is taking place, i.e. physical or with a weapon. Is the officer in control of the situation? Determine if you should assist the officer by using force on the suspects(s). Did the officer ask for help, or are they unable to ask for assistance? Is the officer able to get away to a safe place of cover (in the case of being shot at) until back up arrives? Finally, has the situation gotten to the point that it would be of no use to try and assist the officer, and is it time to save yourself? "Decision making under these conditions is not an easy task. Only you know or have an idea of what you feel you are capable of. Try to stay calm and use good judgment. Do not be afraid to incapacitate or injure a suspect. It very well could save your or the officer's life."(13)

Not every ride-along is going to involve dangerous or critical incidents (though every ride-along potentially involves dangerous or critical incidents). The more ride-alongs you do, and the more consistent you become at doing them, the more confident you will become. The officers will also grow to respect and value having a Chaplain around.

One area where the Chaplain will often be able to work with the officer is in counseling. The Chaplain may be able to invoke confidentiality with the officer. States differ on the laws regarding privileged communication, but one thing they do agree on is that one must be **licensed or ordained** to have privileged communication. Every state has different laws concerning confidentiality, and every denomination has diverse by-laws for their ministers. Make sure you know the laws, and your denominational by-laws and that you have the ability to invoke confidentiality before you try to use it with an officer.

Normally, a state will issue certain statutes identifying the limitations of privileged communications. Typically the first statue requires that the person invoking privileged communication is a clergy person, acting in the capacity of a clergy person. Secondly, the privileged communication must be given to a clergy person acting in their professional capacity as recognized by their denomination. In other words, a random conversation with a clergy person is not necessarily considered privileged. Thirdly, to be a confidential communication, it must be "spiritual" in nature, such as a confession. Finally, the privileged communication must be between two people, without the presence of a third person. If there is a third person present, then there is not this "clergy-penitent" type of privileged communication.

I have always told cops when I am doing ride-alongs with them that anything said in the squad car, stays in the squad car. In other words, anything they say while we are on the ride-along stays between us. I consider everything said in the car as confidential.

There are limits to privileged communication, such as mandated reporting laws. It may be lawfully required to report such things as child or elder abuse, or if the person is a threat to themselves or another person. These laws are also known as "public peril statues." The most important thing is to know what your own state, and your own denomination has to say about privileged communications.

It is essential for officers to be able to speak with the Chaplain confidentially, and off the record. That is one of the advantages of going to the chaplain, over a peer support, or an agency psychiatrist or counselor. This doesn't mean that there may not be times when the chaplain needs to refer out to peer counselors and agency psychiatrists. The nature of the work of a Chaplain is often such that long-term counseling is difficult if not impossible. Most of the counseling done by the Chaplain will be short term, or crisis-oriented counseling. Therefore it is wise to know who you can refer an officer to for long-term help. Obviously you would want to refer them to law enforcement friendly resources.

There is a moral, and Biblical obligation for the Chaplain to be able to keep secrets. The Bible tells us over in Proverbs 25:9, "Debate thy cause with thy neighbor himself and discover not a secret to another." Even if what is being shared is not of a confidential nature, it is important that you don't share with others what you have discussed.

It takes time to build trust among officers that you will keep their confidences. If you prove yourself in even the small things, more officers will begin coming to you for assistance. Even when you do not invoke confidentiality, you must never gossip, spread rumors, or share confidences. Proverbs 11:13 tells us, "A talebearer revealeth secrets: but he that is of a faithful spirit concealeth the matter." Nothing will convince officers their privacy will be honored better than the recommendation of a fellow officer.

If a Chaplain does not keep a confidence it will be found out very quickly. Many years' worth of work can be destroyed by one slip of the tongue. Officers will not trust a Chaplain who reveals secrets told in confidence.

There may be cases where an officer is referred to the Chaplain by his or her supervisor. It is best to tell the supervisor to not expect any written or verbal report in keeping the confidence of the officer. Rather, their supervisor should look to see improvement in the officer's job performance.

CHAPTER 12
A PLUME FOR THE HELMET

The Chaplain works in three areas or "ventions." The first area is prevention. Prevention is stopping something (in this context, something bad) from happening. The second area is called intervention. Intervention is stepping into the midst of a person's crisis, coming alongside of them, and helping them get through the critical first few hours and days. The last area is postvention. Postvention is covered thoroughly in section four of this book. Postvention is picking up the pieces after a critical incident event has happened, and a person's world has seemingly come apart. This goes far beyond just a crisis situation. An example of postvention is helping an officer after you have had to tell them that their daughter will not be coming home because she was killed in a car crash.

Some people will question the authority of the Chaplain to minister to state or federal employees. They may say such things as, "What about the separation of Church and State?" Before we go any further, let's examine why we can be endorsed by law enforcement to do the work of a Chaplain. The first amendment to the constitution says, "Congress shall make no law respecting an establishment of religion, or prohibiting the free exercise thereof; or abridging the freedom of speech, or of the press; or the right of the people peaceably to assemble, and to petition the government for a redress of grievances." (14)

Back in 1971, the Supreme Court addressed the issue of whether a statute or government policy will offend the establishment clause of the first amendment in a case called "Lemon vs. Kurtzman". To quote the court, they said, "First, the statute must have a secular legislative purpose; second, its principal or primary effect must be one that neither advances nor inhibits religion; and finally, the statute must not foster an excessive government entanglement with religion." (15) This has come to be known as the "Lemon Test."

There are certain guidelines that must be followed for a faith-based group to avoid constitutional issues. The Lemon Test does not say that there can be no religious purpose. It does say however that there must be a secular purpose. The courts have so far ruled in favor of allowing faith based programs even if there is a substantial benefit to religion, as long as there is a secular purpose. An example is the prayer room in the Alabama State capitol. In the case of Wallace V.S. Jaffree, Van Zandt V.S. Thompson, Id. At p680. The 7th circuit court of appeals held that the prayer room in the state capitol had the secular purpose of promoting meditation, and thus met the conditions of the Lemon Test.

There was another case challenging a Chaplain program at a hospital. The case was Carter V.S. Broadlawns Medical Center. The 8th circuit court held that the valid secular purpose of the Chaplain program was to help people get well. So we see from these two examples that there can be a religious benefit to a program without violating the Lemon Test. A Chaplain program can exist and function with a government institution, or state run program as long as there is a secular purpose to the program.

There have been more recent cases, and in every case the high courts have upheld the rights of the chaplain programs.

The second prong to the test has to do with promotion of religion. In several cases, the courts have ruled that the fact that a religiously based organization happens to receive an incidental benefit under a government policy doesn't mean that it violates this part of the Lemon Test. If the program's exclusive purpose is to promote a religion, then there would certainly be a problem.

The government is not to have an undue part or entanglement in the religious portion of the organization. There have been cases where the functions of the Chaplain were considered vague and undefined. The courts initially ruled that if the government paid the Chaplain, such as in the case of a state run hospital, the functions and duties of the Chaplain would need to be completely defined, and examined by the government. This was later overturned on appeal, because the government considered their role of overseeing a Chaplain as being entangled in the religious portion of the Chaplain program. If the government has too much involvement, they themselves will cause a failure of the Lemon Test.

The U.S. Supreme Court has consistently rejected attempts to bar public hospitals from keeping Chaplains on their payrolls. One specific example was a challenge made by three atheists. These three atheists challenged a paid Chaplain's position maintained by Polk County's Broadlawns Medical Center in Des Moines, IA. The Supreme Court turned away arguments that spending taxpayer money for a hospital Chaplain's job violated the U.S. Constitution's requirement of the separation of Church and State. The requirements laid out by the 8th Circuit U.S. Court of Appeals did place certain limitations on the position. From these limitations, we can glean four points that a Chaplain program should keep in mind when dealing with issues of Constitutionality. If they follow these four simple guidelines, they should be safe:

1.   The program has a "secular" purpose

2.   Is religiously neutral

3.   Avoids excessive religious entanglement

4.   It has a long standing program, or history (16)

There are those in our society today who would re-write history to suit their own beliefs. Some people are ignorant of our history, and are easily taken in by these revisionists, so it is important for the Chaplain to know something of our heritage. Chaplains have a long rich history in the United States, and this is very well documented.

Chaplains have been involved in the U.S. government since the founding of the nation. There are records indicating that there were Chaplains on the Mayflower. George Washington commissioned Chaplains to serve in the military during the Revolutionary War. After the war, our first president praised the work of the Chaplains, and said they did such an outstanding job he made them a permanent institution and part of our military. Chaplains and chaplain programs have existed from the beginning of our country. They can be seen active in our government for hundreds of years.

Now that we have established the constitutionality of the Chaplain program, we can look at some of the ways the chaplain can help. Many of the issues and problems that face law enforcement officers can be addressed early, before they become problems. If a person is aware of potential hazards ahead, they are better prepared to avoid them, or at least be forewarned so they won't be taken by surprise. By going into law enforcement academies, and teaching classes on self care, stress, the tendency to become cynical, and what the recruit can expect in their law enforcement career, they will be more prepared for what lies ahead of them. "The academy is the best time to train officers about stress because there they are a captive and relatively receptive audience and the information will be of use to them for their entire police careers." (17) By offering this training during the academy, the recruit can take steps to prepare for what lies ahead with their career, and will not be taken off guard. By introducing the recruit to the Chaplain during academy, the young cop will be much more likely to trust the Chaplain and seek them out early when they face crisis situations in their lives and careers.

There should be an emphasis during the training on self-care dealing with stress. The Chaplain should cover the sources of stress, its various manifestations, and the strategies the officer can use to cope with stress. The goals of the training should include instruction how to eliminate stress, and how to deal with a stressful state or circumstances before it leads to other problems. Simply educating the recruits about stress will help reduce the amount of stress they will experience the first year out of academy, and into their career.

An additional benefit of the Chaplain teaching academy classes is that it lowers the stigma associated with going to the Chaplain for help. It raises the visibility and merit of the Chaplain.

At some time shortly before graduation, an academy class for the spouses and family members of the recruits can be taught. The spouses and family members are very important to the officer, and will be either a major source of strength for them, or a source of stress and a hindrance to their career. If the spouses and family members are aware of the stressors and potential issues that come with being an officer, they can be there to help support them. The spouse and family members should be taught about the unique stress involved in police work and the issues that affect most officers. They should be aware of the signs and symptoms of PTSD. And they should be instructed about the demands of being part of a law enforcement family. Some other subjects that may be covered are:

1.   The advantages of being part of a law enforcement family

2.   Being aware of potential problems in a marital/familial relationship and how to address them before they can get out of control

3.   Elimination of stress causing choices and lifestyles

4.   Taking time for each other, and building relationships

5.   Marriage/Familial goals (18)

(More information about Spouse's Academy can be found in chapter 14.)

The Chaplain should be a source of training and information. He or she can host seminars of interest to law enforcement officers in general. There are a number of excellent speakers available who speak to specific law enforcement issues. There are seminars on dealing with law enforcement stress and PTSD; on preparing for the "what ifs" of being an officer, i.e. officer involved shootings, injuries, etc.; law enforcement suicide prevention; and a host of other subjects. The seminars should be on subjects meaningful to the officers, and that they will come out to attend. One very helpful and well attended seminar would be for law enforcement managers on how to deal with the line of duty death funeral. No one wants to see that happen, but reality is it does happen, and most departments are not ready to deal with it.

The last course of training the Chaplain can offer is for those officers that are facing retirement. "Retirement can be an exceptionally difficult experience for some officers. Often they need practical assistance with financial and other matters as well as help with stress-related problems." (19) Since we realize that a large number of retired law enforcement officers end up taking their own lives, a portion of the training should be on suicide prevention. An officer's retirement is a very big life change, and should not be taken lightly by the Chaplain. As Allen R. Kates, the author of Cop Shock says about retirement, "Everything he or she is and has worked for seems to suddenly come to an end. This may result in depression and trigger memories of traumatic experiences long buried. An officer must prepare for a successful retirement." (20)

As a Chaplain, you can and will make a difference in the life of officer's and in the department. Much of the difference you make will depend on you – how much time and investment you are willing to make – how visible in the department you are – and how much you care about and for the officers that you are responsible for. God will give the increase, but He expects you to be His feet and hands.

SECTION IV
THE CHAPLAIN'S ROLE

CHAPTER 13
TAKE MY HAND

Matthew 14:22-32, "*Immediately Jesus made the disciples get into the boat and go on ahead of him to the other side, while he dismissed the crowd. After he had dismissed them, he went up on a mountain by himself to pray. When evening came, he was there alone, but the boat was already a considerable distance from land, buffeted by the waves because the wind was against it.*

During the fourth watch of the night Jesus went out to them, walking on the lake. When the disciples saw him walking on the lake, they were terrified. "It's a ghost," they said, and cried out in fear.

But Jesus immediately said to them: "Take courage! It is I. Don't be afraid."

"Lord, if it's you," Peter replied, "tell me to come to you on the water."

"Come," he said.

Then Peter got down out of the boat, walked on the water and came toward Jesus. But when he saw the wind, he was afraid and, beginning to sink, cried out "Lord, save me!"

"Immediately Jesus reached out his hand and caught him. "You of little faith," he said, "why did you doubt?"

And when they climbed into the boat, the wind died down."(1)

Life is like a journey. We travel through each day of life, hoping, planning, looking forward to what lies ahead. We enjoy the present and look in fond memory of the past. At some point in every person's life, we go through a tragic loss.   Our lives during those times seem to be in such turmoil that it seems we are in the midst of a storm. During the most severe storms of life, when our lives seem to be falling apart, we look for strength in those around us, who can help us brave the storms.

In the gospel narrative of the New Testament in the Bible, there are two different storms mentioned.   In the first storm, Jesus and his disciples are crossing a great expanse of water. Remember that many of Jesus' disciples had been fishermen all of their lives, and knew very well how to handle their boat in a storm. Jesus had gone below deck to get some rest. He was asleep when this storm hit. The disciples did all they could fighting against this storm, but for all of their skills and abilities, their ship was about to sink. Some of them, out of desperation, called down to Jesus for help. They screamed out "Don't you care that we are all about to die?"

Jesus came up from below deck and spoke to the storm. He said, "Peace, be still" and the storm stopped.

The other storm mentioned in the gospels, finds the disciples again out at sea. This time Jesus was not with them, because he had sent them on ahead of him. They were fighting the storm when they saw Jesus coming towards them walking on the water.   Peter, in his amazement, said, "If that's really you, then allow me to come to you."

Jesus said, "Come on, then!"

Peter stepped out of the boat and began walking out on the water as if it was solid ground. Before he got too far, he looked around and saw the waves crashing around him: he heard the wind howling, and realized he was in the middle of this huge violent storm, and he began to sink. He cried out for help.

Jesus reached out and took him by the hand. He pulled him up out of the raging sea that was about to drown him.

132

Then, Jesus led Peter by the hand through the raging storm back to the boat. When they got into the boat, the storm immediately stopped.

As Chaplains, we are often referred to as God with skin on. We are called to represent God, and be as Jesus to people in the most severe crisis of their lives. We come to them to bring them peace and calm in the midst of the storm.

One description of what a law enforcement Chaplain does is, "they are here to save those who save others." They are often called to do the job that no one else wants to do. They may deliver death notifications to an individual person, or be asked to minister to a large group of people. "Chaplains assist entire communities when tragedy and loss have left no one untouched." (2)

Chaplains are probably called out to crisis situations surrounding death more often than any other kind of call. In most of those situations, it is not as important what we say, as it is just being there. "There is really nothing that anyone can say that is adequate to the pain and suffering of deep personal loss. To say to another, "I know exactly how you feel," is always false, and tends to cut the other off from expressing his or her feelings." (3) The work of the Chaplain could be described as a gift of ministry of presence – not pressure.

So many people say, "I don't know what to say to a person who has lost a loved one." So instead, they avoid the person, and don't say anything.

People most appreciate the Chaplains presence, and willingness to listen. When you arrive on the scene of a crisis situation, don't be in a hurry to begin talking. Take the time to listen to where the victims are, and what they need. "What makes a profound difference is someone who will stand near, listen to the cries of anguish and pain. And by their presence, assure those who need to know that indeed someone cares." (4)

The Chaplain doesn't have all the answers, and should never spout scripture or clichés. There is often a nugget of truth in clichés – and we know that scripture can be healing if used in the right way. However, using clichés when a person is in crisis, or quoting scripture because you don't know what else to say is not helpful. There is an old saying, "Better caught than taught." In other words, often times these scriptures are a lot more helpful and healing when the Holy Spirit brings them to people, than when people use them in the form of a cliché. Here are a few cliché's that you should never use on a person in crisis:

"Remember, all things work together for good"

"God moves in mysterious ways"

"It must have been God's will"

"God never gives us more than we can handle"

"God helps those who help themselves"

"I know just how you feel".

When you have just lost a child, you don't feel like "God never gives you more than you can handle".

A few more clichés you should never use include, "God must have needed him more than you do"; "You have to be strong now for your kids"; or one of the worst "God must have needed another flower for His garden in heaven".

Probably one of the most misused, and most hurtful clichés is "If you need anything just call me." They have already asked for help, which is why you are there. You should never require a victim to ask for help a second time. You could say something like, "I will call you tomorrow; please let me know what you need me to do for you." Then make sure that you do call, or better yet stop by.

Instead of using clever platitudes, that really don't make anyone feel better except the person saying them; listen without trying to give answers or interjecting your own survivor stories. "We may all raise the question "why" following a tragedy. But our deepest need is not for answers, because, in reality, our most painful questions have no answers. Any attempt to deliver cheap answers or religious doctrine is less than helpful. Ultimately, those cheap answers and doctrinal utterances hurt the victims and the Chaplaincy itself." (5)

When the time is right, it is O.K to say something like, "This must seem like more hurt than you can stand to bear all at once" or "If I were you I would probably really feel like crying right now". Give the person permission to grieve, and cry. You may be the one person who will allow them to cry without judging them.

There may be times, especially after an awful homicide or suicide when you need to re-direct the victim's emotions. In the case of a suicide, they may be so angry and so intensely concentrating on the fact that their loved one committed suicide, that they can't move beyond that to simply mourn their loss. You may at those times say something like, "It is not important right now how they died. For now, just concentrate on the fact that they are gone."

Death notifications:

Imagine it is dark night, about 0200 (2 a.m.). The house is isolated, quiet and dark. Suddenly there is a loud knocking at the door...

"Sheriff's Department!"

Slowly the door opens..."Mrs. Jones? Mrs. Jones, I'm (insert your name). I have some very important information for you. May I come in?"

"Is anyone else home?...Why don't you sit over here?... Mrs. Jones, do you have a daughter named Jennifer?... Is her birthday March 2nd, 1991?... Mrs. Jones, I need to tell you that your daughter was killed tonight by a drunk driver."

You've just changed a person's life forever. Receiving this kind of information feels like getting hit in the gut with a sledge hammer. Raw emotions may totally take control; other times a sense of numbness sweeps over a person.

No one enjoys delivering bad news, but it is often part of an officer's responsibilities. In the absence of a Chaplain, the responsibility for conducting a death notification falls to the law enforcement officer. Very few officers do death notifications well, and if given the opportunity they most all gladly defer this duty to the Chaplain.

Most officers know it is much better to have the assistance of a chaplain when delivering this kind of message.

Officers are trained to be in control at all times. It is extremely difficult to control someone else's emotions. Chaplains are trained to deal with people's emotions, and can often stay with a family long after the officer has to leave. They have time to ensure the family has a support system of friends and family, and can answer questions about what happens next, such as coroner procedures and funeral homes. The officer can go to the next call knowing the family is in good hands.

There are steps to take to ensure a competent death notification:

Never make a death notification by phone.

Verbally confirm identity. Make sure you have correct information. Verify that you have the correct name and address of the person you are notifying from the person or agency requesting you to make the death notification. Read back what you think they have told you. It is uncomfortable enough, without showing up at the wrong door, or getting a name wrong.

When you arrive at the address, don't park right in front of the house, especially if you are in a marked car. I usually park a couple of houses away or better yet next to a vacant lot. You don't want all of the neighbors running up to the home to see what is going on.

Gain entry. Never give the notification on the front porch, standing in the doorway, or through a locked door (screen or otherwise). If someone collapses behind a locked door, it may be very difficult to help them.

Quickly assess and steer the person to a soft room with cushioned chairs. Sit them in a chair where their knees are higher than their waist. Some people become violent or run when highly emotional. You have more control if they can't get up quickly. If they do pass out (it has happened to me on several occasions), it is less likely they will fall and hurt themselves.

Ask if anyone else is home. It can be very dangerous to tell a person that their loved one has died if the person screams and falls to their knees - and their protective spouse comes running out of another room to see you standing there. Get everyone in the room so you don't have to make repeated notifications. You may have to make notifications to other family members as they arrive, which may cause waves of emotion to sweep over the family.

Confirm the relationship by saying something like, "Is your husband John Smith?" And, "What is his birthday?" Verify the information you have with the person you are notifying. You should have a name and a birth date to verify you are notifying the correct person.

When you are satisfied that you are dealing with the family member (next of kin) that you are supposed to notify, get right to the point. Say something like, "I need to tell you that your son was killed tonight". Don't make small talk, or lead up to what you need to say. Don't say something like, "I'm sorry. I have some bad news for you. Something terrible has happened." This only prolongs their pain, and with every sentence their blood pressure rises along with their adrenaline. Trying to prepare a person for bad news doesn't make it easier for them to hear it. The kindest thing you can do is be direct. Use words such as dead or killed. Don't say "we are sorry," or that "we have bad news." Tell them something like, "Mrs. Smith, I need to tell you your husband was killed tonight in a car crash." It is far more merciful to be straight to the point. If you use vague words such as, "a critical incident", or "they have passed away", it is not clear that their loved one has died, and once again it will be more traumatic than coming right out with the notification.

Be prepared for ANY reaction.

This is important - The notification should be completed within a couple of minutes of entering the home. If it takes longer than that, you are adding undue stress to an already stressful situation.

The next of kin will often ask what happened. Be prepared to share limited information. Absolute honesty is not always the best way to handle things. They don't need to know that their loved one's "guts were all over the freeway," or that "they suffered horribly before they died."

Be specific but tactful. Use soft but plain language. Give no reason for false hopes. They will want to know if you are certain it is their loved one. Be very direct and confident in the information you are sharing.

Don't rush off. Try to make sure they have some support in place before leaving. Offer to call a relative, a neighbor, or clergy to be with them.

When an officer dies, the notification to the next of kin needs to be done as quickly as possible. Local media is usually the second to know of a line of duty death, and they will compete to "break the news first." It is imperative the notification team be assembled and get to the next of kin very quickly.

The death notification team for a law enforcement line of duty death should consist of the following:

1.   The department chaplain.
2.   The chief/sheriff or their representative.
3.   A Close friend(s) of the officer.

The team needs to arrive together to make the death notification. Deep emotional reactions can be expected, so the department chaplain is the logical choice to make the official notification in the presence of the agency representatives. Decide who will make the notification before arriving at the next of kin's location. As soon as the family sees this group coming, they will know the news is not good.

Secondary notifications include the officer's parents, grandparents, brothers and sisters. Also notify the spouse's parents, grandparents, brothers and sisters, and any others the family requests. Every notification should be made in person whenever possible.

One of the first decisions that need to be made for the family is who will be the assigned liaison officer. This should be a personal friend of the family. This officer will convey the family's wishes and be a go-between for the family and the department. They will remain with the family at all times, providing security, transportation, and information. The chaplain should be available to the family and the liaison officer.

All of the officers in the department need to be notified. This should either be done in person or by phone. Close friends of the officer should be told in person.

A teletype needs to be sent to allied agencies notifying them of the death. Local news will make the officer down report on TV and radio saying, "The name of the officer will not be released until the next of kin has been notified." This will be a very stressful time for the entire agency, and spouses and families of the officers. Advise all officers on duty to call their spouse/family and let them know they are okay.

Death notifications are never easy. Following these guidelines will help, but nothing will take away the "sting" of telling someone their loved one is not coming home.

Any time there is a major loss, such as the death of a loved one, there is an impact stage. When you deliver a death notification, you make an impact on a person that is going to change their life forever. Normal reactions at this stage range from shock, to disbelief, anger to sadness. In fact, you can expect to see almost any emotion or no emotion at all. I once had a person tell me, "Thank you very much. Now, can I get back to my ball game?"

Shortly after the impact stage, the person experiencing the crisis will begin to go into a recoil stage. Again, there may be a whole gauntlet of emotions. The person will often go into denial, saying such things as, "There must be some mistake". They will be home soon."

The goal at this point is to get the person to move past the denial stage to a point of acceptance. In talking with the person, pay attention to their language. When they begin using a past tense in their conversation about their deceased loved one, e.g. "they used to", "he was", etc. instead of "they do", or "he is" they will have moved into acceptance.

Eventually they will move into a recovery phase, where they will begin to be able to function again. They will never be the same as they were before the loss, so we can't tell them they will get back to normal. Instead, they will come to a point where they have a new normal. The pain of loss may never totally go away, but it will decrease, and it will get easier to bear.

Line of Duty Death Funerals:

Line of duty deaths (LODD) are by far one of the most difficult, and demanding roles for a chaplain. The next few pages give some guidelines and suggestions in not only preparing for, but conducting the service. Ideally the department will have a Standard Operating Procedures (S.O.P.) manual with the LODD funeral all spelled out. The reality is most departments don't have this, or the S.O.P. is so old and out of date that it is not very useful.

Rule number 1 for a line of duty death: Don't let the Chief decide when to hold the funeral. They will almost always want to have the funeral service within two or three days. They will make this decision based on emotion, not logic. They will say "The family needs closure". Chiefs are decision makers. Their heart is in the right place, they want to make things easier on the family, but it is very difficult to put together a service honoring an officer in just 2 or 3 days.

Ideally, the funeral should take place about 6 days after the death. A really good outline to follow goes like this.

Day 0 – Day of officer's death. Multiple notifications need to be done.

Day 1-4 Meetings and planning. The department chaplain should be at as many of these as possible. He or she should be part of the planning team.

Day 5   Morning walk through/rehearsal

          Afternoon viewing / vigil service

Day 6 Funeral and Internment Honors Ceremony

Day 7 Planning team debriefing

The family's wishes should be paramount. They should be allowed to grieve without any concerns for the first day. However, they need to be prepared to meet with the chaplain and various members of the funeral operation command staff the day after. There is a lot to be accomplished in a very short time. This should be done very gently, but many of the preparations need to begin immediately.

Some families will not want a big line of duty death funeral service. Honor the wishes of the family, with a small personal funeral service if that is what they wish. However, let them know that there are a lot of grieving officers out there that will also want to pay their respects. Therefore, there will also be a separate memorial service for these officers. This will be done for the department, but they are invited to attend, and seats will be saved for the family in the front rows.

For the memorial service, you can normally expect several thousand officers to be in attendance. It is disrespectful to these officers, many of whom may have traveled several hours, to have the service in a church or building much too small to accommodate them. Every effort should be made to have the memorial service in a church or building big enough to accommodate all of the officers. This may be a very large local church, or sports arena, etc.

There are several roles or positions to be filled in order to properly perform a LODD funeral.

1. <u>Funeral Operations Coordinator (FOC):</u> Responsible for the entire funeral operation.

Normally this position should be at least a Lieutenant level due to the nature of the people to be handled.

2. <u>Chaplain:</u> The Chaplain works in close concert with the FOC to insure all phases of planning are complete and will work with the family and agency. If the Chaplain is not conducting the service, they will become the liaison between the family, the department, and the clergy.

3. <u>Liaison Officer:</u> Remains with the family at all times. Security, transportation, and liaison between FOC and the family.

4.   Division Contact: From the department the deceased person worked at. Provides liaison between the commander, fellow employees, and the FOC.

5.   Travel coordinator: Arranging and coordinating travel or lodging. Many family members will be coming from out of town. The travel coordinator will help make sure the family from out of town is taken care of and not harassed.

6.   Traffic supervisor: Coordinates moving of vehicles involved in the funeral. From the home to the church; from the church to the cemetery; from the cemetery to reception, etc.

7.   Ceremonial Unit Supervisors: Responsible for all ceremonial rites, such as taps, 21 gun salute, bag pipes, fly over, riderless horse, and flag folding.

8.   Medial Supervisor: This will likely be a PIO (public information officer) used to dealing with reporters. They are responsible for press releases; media at the funeral and reception, and how much or little exposure do the family get to the media.

Other things to think about for the actual service:

The service itself should last about an hour and 15 minutes to 1 ½ hrs. No more than that, or people begin to drift away.

The master of ceremonies (usually the Chaplain) needs to watch out for eulogists. Some of them will get up and find out they like talking. I never recommend an open mic at a large funeral such as for a LODD because it is too easy to lose control.

Each eulogist should be told in advance they have 3 to 5 minutes.

Basically, the service should look something like this time wise:

Minister   20 minutes
Eulogies   26 minutes
    (4 eulogists speaking for 4 minutes each, plus a couple of minutes each to get to the microphone, comes out to about 26 minutes.)
Music   4 songs 17 minutes
Slide show video 7 minutes
        Total 70 minutes
+ 5 minutes for unforeseen circumstances and delays. This comes out to exactly 1 hr 15 minutes.

Not all of the people that come to a funeral service will be officers, so it is really nice if the master of ceremonies can take a moment to explain the various honors. You can spend a little time talking about the significance of the folding of the flag; the riderless horse; gun salute, etc.

Normally the casket is draped with a flag. This flag is folded either at the church service or at the grave side and presented by the chief to the family. The state police department may also present a state flag. There may be circumstances where you have a fiancé, or a blended family. You may want to consider presenting more than one American Flag, e.g. one to the mother and one to the fiancé.

There are some Issues that need to be addressed in line of duty death funerals: Ideally these would be considered and put in writing before there is a LODD.

1. Funding, who pays for what? How much will the department pick up, and what bills will the family get stuck with?
2. Will a trust fund be set up? By whom?
3. Collection of personal and agency property.
4. Folding and presentation of National Flag.
5. Selection of the family liaison officer.
6. Strategic Planning Team Members and responsibilities of each.

7. Primary Coordinator Responsibilities including:
   a. Personnel
   b. Logistics
   c. Traffic
   d. Church
   e. Ushers
   f. Pall bearers
   g. Media
   h. Honor Guard
   i. Honors
   j. Internment
8. Church Events
9. Motorcade planning from and to all locations
10. Internment Events
11. Agency informational meetings
12. Viewing/Vigil considerations
13. Religious and cultural issues
14. unwanted attendees
15. What if there are multiple line of duty deaths at the same time?
16. Day after services debriefings for strategic planning team.

(Thank you to John Cooley with Police USA for his contribution to the information in this chapter on line of duty death funeral services).

Much of the focus of the department heads will be on the funeral service for the week following the line of duty death of an officer. There are other things going on during the week that also need to be taken care of, as well as following the service.

There should be several debriefings or CISMs taking place. The first should be for the ground zero crew. These are the officers that were at the scene immediately following the death. They should be allowed to debrief together.

There should be another CISM that takes care of all of the peripheral people including officers that had some part in the call. These would include dispatchers that were on duty at the time, and others.

There should be another CISM for anyone from the department, or involved with the call such as paramedics, nurses, etc.

Don't neglect the spouses of the officers. They too have been traumatized by the fact it could have been their husband or wife that was killed.

These all need to take place during the few days following the death.

There also needs to be a debriefing for the strategic planning team where they can express their feelings, and also talk about what worked and what didn't during the planning of the funeral, and performing the service etc. This may need to be two separate meetings.

Just because the funeral is over doesn't mean the family now magically has closure. The department needs to adopt this family as part of their own from now on. That means inviting them to events, parties, etc. Don't leave them out. This also means following up with them at holidays, anniversaries, birthdays of the deceased, etc. The Chaplain may be the person to remind the department to not forget this family. At the very least a card from the chief and the department should be sent at all of these times.

During the week after the death, the family will be inundated with visitors, friends, and family. After the funeral this will drop off significantly. After the first month, it often stops all together.

Most times, the family will welcome seeing people from their loved ones department. Officers shouldn't feel like they are imposing, or intruding if they drop by just to say hi and how things are going 6 months or a year after the death.

It takes a special person, selected by God to be effective as a Chaplain. It also takes training, and preparation. Most pastors or ministers, who are not called to be Chaplains, will not be able to do the work that God has called the Chaplain to. They don't know what to say, when to say it, or when to be quiet and listen.

As a Chaplain, you are being called to a very unique and special kind of ministry. Chaplains go where the church cannot go, across the crime scene tape. Chaplains, are going to be sent out to people that are in crisis, whose lives are in the midst of a storm. It is up to you as a Chaplain, to take these people by the hand, just as Jesus took Peter by the hand, and lead them through the stormy tempest and back to the boat where they will be safe.

CHAPTER 14
MARRIAGE HELP

L aw Enforcement Officers have a higher than average rate of divorce. They may come to the Chaplain to address marriage issues they are experiencing. Chaplains need to have some training in this area. It is very advisable that they take a course in marriage and family counseling, and read all they can get their hands on about the subject. The more training and education you have in this area, the better resource, and more help you will be to the officers that come to you. This section will give some helpful tips, some things to suggest and to try.

One thing that can be done to help officers proactively in their family and their marriage is to encourage them to get involved in community activities. These can be such things as youth athletics, or charitable organizations. Officers can be coaches, or referees in youth leagues. "Police will get balance in their lives and citizens will better understand the police. A cooperative attitude will grow on both sides." (6) Many officers find fulfillment in working as a scoutmaster, and at the same time can make a real difference in children's lives. This kind of volunteer work may take some time away from the family, but it will keep the officer's focus on reality, not just on what he or she sees on the streets every day. In the long run, this will be a huge benefit to the officer's family.

Chaplains can conduct something called a "Spouse's Academy". Many departments have started offering these academies as a way to introduce the wives and husbands of rookie cops to the law enforcement culture. The basic structure of a Spouses Academy would look something like this: Introductions with an icebreaking/sharing time; the role of the chaplain; basic cop culture; experiences shared by current spouses of cops; a nice lunch and "get to know you" activity. The one rule is "no cops allowed". Expect mostly women in this group typically, but be ready to accommodate some men as well.

The officer should make a real effort to have his or her spouse attend a spouse's academy. Spousal academies "will help them learn about the department first hand. Spouses don't understand the department and often have a biased opinion after hearing officers gripe." (7) Spousal academies are a great way to get law enforcement spouses together so they can meet each other, build relationships, and gain support from one another. This camaraderie will also help the spouses feel more like they are part of the law enforcement family: like they belong, rather than feeling like an outsider looking in.

A good marriage takes lots of hard work. It takes time, effort and commitment from both partners to make it successful. Here are seven suggestions for creating a happy marriage:

1.   Set aside time for each other. Everyone today lives busy lives. In fact in American life and society it is becoming more and more expected that people will have a number of demands, commitments, and responsibilities. In the midst of our busy-ness, and pressure to achieve, our marriages often get pushed aside "for more important" things. A couple needs to make the time to be together, and build and nurture their marriage. They need to have dates together, reserve special times to be alone with each other, and even just spend a lazy afternoon together talking. If there are kids involved, set aside a day once a month as a family day so the children can spend quality as

well as quantity time with both parents. Be sure to maintain a good balance in time commitments.

2.   Listen to one another. With shift work, and the officer having his or her weekend in the middle of the week, it may take an effort to actually find time to talk. Keep the lines of communication open. At the same time the spouse should realize that sometimes their marriage partner may need quiet time just to process their day. Allow them this time, but be sure to come back together later and do marriage-building activities.

3.   Confront issues before they become a problem. Take the time to examine issues together. Try to identify the specific problem, and not just be "angry" about everything in general. Learn to forgive each other for shortcomings, and work through the difficult times by communicating openly but at the same time being gentle with each other. Remember the Bible says that true love always protects. If what you have to say is hurtful, consider if it really needs to be said. "One of the best ways to overcome potential problems is to look for signs that it is developing and deal with it while it is manageable. Be aware! Avoid letting the tendencies that plague police relationships become realities." (8)

4.   If you have a complaint, be ready with a constructive suggestion about how to fix it. This doesn't mean using the "suggestion" as a weapon to inflict more harm during an argument. It also doesn't mean the cop controlling their partner. Police work and marriage are two totally different things, and should be treated accordingly. The Chaplain should be able to help the couple with building conflict resolution skills. The couple should work on not having a negative attitude with each other. Note that a spouse's spoken satisfaction with their spouse's law enforcement career carries a lot of weight. Most officers need approval from their spouses, and have a lot less

stress when they receive positive affirmations of the job they are doing on a regular basis.

5.   Avoid always being the one in control at home. This may be tough for the officer who is used to being in control all of the time on the job.   No one wants to be controlled all of the time, or have someone else make all of the decisions for us. Sometimes the spouse who is not an officer needs to set a course and stick to it, rather than giving control over to their husband or wife. Set goals as a couple, and work together to achieve these goals.   One way to do this is to take turns planning the (at least) once a month date night.

6.   Be in touch with how each other feels.   The partner that is the officer needs to be aware of the needs of his or her spouse to be loved and cared for. Feelings need to be recognized and affirmed. Cops tend to shut down their emotions while on the job. It is a common issue for a cop to not be able to turn their emotions back on at home. Don't play down the feelings of your spouse. Being able to share concerns and ideas with each other is good for the relationship and will foster closeness and companionship.

7.   Have a good support network. These can be such things as good safe relationships with friends, being part of support groups, family, church and community activities. If there are still issues that are not getting resolved then the couple needs to feel comfortable seeking counseling. Some couples think that going to counseling is a sign of weakness. Reassure them it is actually a sign of a healthy and strong relationship that is growing and maturing. There is no stigma in asking for help when you need it.

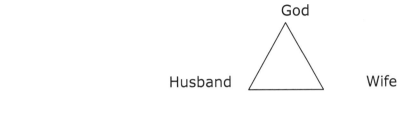

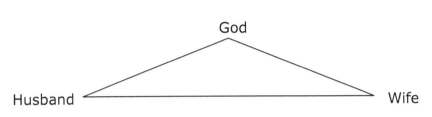

This is a diagram I have found useful, especially when dealing with couples who consider themselves Christians. As the diagram illustrates, our closeness to each other as husband and wife has a direct relation to our closeness to God. The first triangle shows a couple with a good marriage, with God at the center of their marriage. The lower triangle shows how as a couple drifts apart from each other; they also drift farther and farther from God. The farther they move away from each other, the farther they end up moving away from God. God is constant – He never moves. It is the husband and wife that do the moving.

Some of your goals in marriage counseling may look like this sample list:

1.   Identify and understand the specific issues that are creating the marital difficulties

2.   Teach the couple how to communicate constructively

3.   Teach problem solving and decision making techniques

4.   Help the couple understand the counseling relationship with the Chaplain

5.   Help both partners express their frustrations, disappointments, and desires for the future

6.   Instill hope for the marriage
7.   Keep the husband and wife together
8.   Help the couple set goals for their marriage

When the Chaplain helps to set goals in counseling, whether it is with an officer, the officer's spouse, or their family, they know the direction the counseling needs to take. Goal setting helps the Chaplain to have direction, and purpose in counseling, and helps the couple see progress as they reach goals that have been set. (9)

Pre-marital counseling is always an excellent idea. It not only helps the couple enter the marriage commitment with their eyes open, and knowing what to expect, it also helps the couple to not have a fear of seeking counseling in the future.   If the pre-marital counseling is a positive experience for both partners, statistics show they will be more likely to seek counseling if their marriage becomes troubled later on. They will also be more likely to seek counseling for other familial problems they may encounter. "Providing services to families of officers can help to prevent and reduce the stress-related difficulties family members may experience, limit the stress that family members may cause the officer in the family, and help family members become a source of support for the officer." (10)

These are just a few tips. Nothing substitutes for a good education. There are good training classes in counseling. You may even be able to audit classes at your local Bible College for a small fee if you are not looking to complete a degree program.

CHAPTER 15
LAW ENFORCEMENT OFFICERS AND SUICIDE

The occurrence of suicide among law enforcement officers is very high. Often this is due to the excessive amount of stress they endure on the job, followed by a time of deep depression. The depression may be brought on by such things as marital problems, or a relationship gone bad; excessive isolation or separation; financial problems; prolonged illness; a loss of self esteem or of a good self image; or guilt from some illegal activity. Suicide among officers is especially prevalent after their retirement.

More men tend to commit suicide than women later in life. "Part of the reason more men than women kill themselves in advanced years seems to be that men have a much more difficult time adjusting to the dependency that old age brings." (11) Law enforcement officers have been taught to always be in control. There is often a feeling of loss of control among retired officers.

When dealing with a suicidal person, it is important to get help. Don't try to do it all on your own. Even if you are professionally trained, if a person is really determined to commit suicide, and they are a danger to themselves, they need to be psychologically evaluated for their own safety. If you can't get them to contact someone for help, you may have to call 911 (You can always apologize later.)

There are signs and symptoms a person will typically have if they are suicidal. In the majority of cases, suicide is not spontaneous, even if it appears to be. There are exceptions to this rule, especially in the case of teenagers, but very few people decide in an instant to kill themselves. It is normally a long drawn out process, often over the course of weeks, or even months before the act. Some of the signs or symptoms to watch for are listed here:

1.   Depression seems to be one of the most common keys. A person will most often commit suicide because of some kind of pain, which is usually in some way related to depression. The pain may be real or imagined. Be aware that if a person seems depressed for a long period of time, and suddenly seems content, at peace, or even happy, they may have come to a decision to commit suicide. Often when a depressed person decides to commit suicide, they figure out how they are going to do it, and set a time and date, e.g. "...with my gun in my room on Mother's day at noon". At that point they will come to peace with themselves and with the idea of ending it all.

2.   Some of the symptoms of depression will be visible, such as a lack of energy or motivation; being withdrawn; unable to concentrate; being easily made to cry; no longer caring about physical fitness, or their appearance; etc.

3.   A suicidal person may mention suicide to someone. If a person mentions this to you, take it seriously, and gently ask them if they have been considering suicide. It's very important to use the word suicide. Many people try to use softer language, or ask if they want to hurt themselves. Most people don't like pain, and don't want to cause themselves more pain. They want the pain to stop. Often, just asking them very specifically about suicide and making them feel at ease about talking about it will relieve much of their stress and anxiety.

4.   Alcohol is a very common element in suicide. Alcohol is a depressant drug, and can make the symptoms of depression much worse. If a person starts drinking, or begins drinking much more than they normally do, this can be a sign of something eating away at them. They may be self medicating.

5.   They may begin combining tranquilizers with alcohol, trying to numb their pain.

6.   Especially in the case of a law enforcement officer, they may become reckless, and accident-prone. This may be most evident in their service vehicle. You may notice them taking unnecessary risks, or being more reckless than usual.

7.   They may write letters to their close friends expressing their wishes if something were to happen to them.

8.   They may suddenly have an interest in writing or updating their will.

9.   Often a person who is seriously considering suicide will try to make amends with anyone they have hurt or offended, and begin giving away their most prized possessions.

10.   They may begin playing with their gun, pointing it at themselves or others for no reason.

These are all symptoms of a suicidal person. It doesn't mean that they are going to harm themselves, but it is possible. The best way to find out whether a person is thinking of killing themselves is to simply ask them.

To reiterate, when a person says something like, "I should just kill myself", or "I wish I was never born", ask them gently if they are thinking of killing themselves. It may have been just a fleeting thought, and they may have no intentions of doing themselves harm.

There is an escalation of suicide. The lower scale may start with a person having the fleeting thought of suicide. This may show a very low lethality rate. The high end of the scale may be a person with a gun in the next room that they are going to use as soon as you leave. This is a high lethality. If a person says they are thinking about suicide, you should ask them if they have thought about how they will do it, where they will do it, and when. If they know how they will kill themselves, e.g. with a gun; where they will do it, e.g. laying down in their bed; and when they will do it, e.g. tomorrow, at 6:00 P.M; there is a very high lethality probability and you need to get them immediate help. The following diagram maps out the scale of lethality with 1-2 being the lowest risk, and 9-10 being an immediate, significant risk:

"I know when I will kill myself"
9   Plan in place, how, where, and when
    Call 911

8 "I know where I would kill myself"

7   Get professional help for them

6 You can always apologize tomorrow

5 "I know how I would kill myself"

4   Take this very seriously

3 Use effective listening skills

2 "I want to kill myself"

1   Take this seriously, but consider the circumstances (12)

Suicide prevention is a very important aspect of the Chaplain's responsibility. Of course the best way to prevent it is to deal with it before it ever becomes an issue. The best time to do that is before the officer ever gets out of the academy. As mentioned in the previous chapter, part of the class on self-care and stress management should cover suicide prevention.

As the Chaplain goes about their duties, they can be aware and watchful of officers showing suicidal symptoms. One of the easiest ways to do this is to look for people who seem to be hurting. People who are in misery, physically, or mentally – real or imagined are the ones who will likely be considering suicide. So basically, we could say it is misery reduction. All Chaplains should have the skills necessary to look for a person in misery. "Most of the sources of misery come under the heading of stress. We all face stress, of course; it is when we are no longer able to cope with it that it becomes truly misery-making to the extent that it is life-threatening." (13)

A person who is suicidal goes through a thought process that leads them to the point where they think there is no other way out than suicide. They feel they can no longer handle the situation, because it is too painful. They are simply miserable. Their reasoning becomes impaired, and hopelessness begins to set in. It is like all they can see is the suicide. It is so much in their face they can't see any other alternative.

When working with a suicidal person, very often the most important thing we can do is to be there and listen. As most other critical incident calls, often it is not so much what we say, but our being there and helping the victim tell us about their pain that is most healing for them. "The most important thing, when dealing with someone in trouble or emotional stress, is not that you can say something to them that might be helpful, but that you can listen to them. Nothing you can say can heal them; but something they might say to you could help them begin to heal themselves." (14) Most of your side of the conversation should be encouraging them to talk more, to think about what they are telling you, and showing that you are truly listening and understanding what they are saying. If they talk about reasons to die long enough, they will begin to give reasons to live.

Don't be afraid to ask for help when dealing with a suicidal person. Know your own limits, and don't try to do more than you are able, depending on where they are at on the scale of lethality. Remember, a life may hang in the balance depending on your actions, so don't just "wing it". If you have time, get a professional involved.

There are certain steps, and things you can do when ministering to or counseling a suicidal person. Depending on the lethality scale, if law enforcement is not involved, that should be a priority, especially if the loss of life is eminent.

Be yourself when talking to a suicidal person, being aware of your own feelings and emotions. If you try to be overly clinical, you will seem phony, and it won't feel natural to you or the person you are counseling. If you try to act like an expert, or try to solve all of their problems for them, it will probably be resented.

Never be argumentative with a suicidal person. That doesn't mean you have to agree with everything they say, but don't feel like you have to be right. Talk frankly and openly with the person, but make sure your voice has a caring tone.

Be aware of body language in the person you are counseling. Don't be afraid to use a touch on the hand, or shoulder, to convey concern for them. If they pull away, and obviously don't want to be touched, don't push this. Touch can be very calming, reassuring, and comforting when done in the right way. However, if they are conveying to you that they don't want to be touched, then don't touch. A simple touch for someone who wants it is enough to bring them back into a better state of mind, and bring things back into focus.

Many times, suicidal people have lost all sense of hope. Try to find some way to provide them hope and a reason to live. It might be as simple initially as telling them that their beloved dog or cat would starve to death if they weren't there to take care of them. Help them find reasons to live, by being a good listener first. Eventually, you will pick up reasons they want to live. Most people who are suicidal will begin to show signs of being ambivalent i.e. they want to die, but they also want to live.

As on all critical incident calls, don't be in a hurry. Take your time with the person. They will have a hard time "keeping a gun to their head" for a long period of time. The adrenaline and energy they feel just before committing suicide is also very draining, and will eventually tire them out. Try to discharge their emotions, giving them a vent to relieve some of the pressure.

If in spite of everything you do and say, the person still takes their own life, get help for you! Don't put it off, or think that you can "handle it". (15)

In cases where you arrive after a completed suicide, it can be helpful to the survivors to explain to them about the lethality scale of suicide. Explain to them that there very likely was not anything they could have done to prevent the suicide, and that the person was probably contemplating and planning the suicide for some time. In most cases, the family will recognize, in hindsight, the symptoms that were present leading up to the suicide. Very often I hear on scene something to this effect, "He was really depressed and having a hard time until about a month ago, then all of a sudden he seemed to snap out of it, and he was his old self again. He seemed to get better. I had no idea there was anything wrong." As noted earlier, most people come to a point of being at peace when they complete a suicide plan in their mind, often weeks or months before the actual act.

There may be strong emotions among survivors when they have lost a loved one to suicide. Be willing and ready to hear and accept these feelings. They may be angry at God, and take it out on you as His representative. Let them know that whatever they are feeling is O.K.

It is important to ignore "taboos." Every culture has its own taboo surrounding suicide. It is important that the bereaved be able to talk about their pain, and work through it. Any taboos about suicide that stand in the way of the bereaved working through their grief and beginning the healing process should be ignored or consciously denied.

There is no evidence to prove that suicide notes are any more truthful than other forms of communication. If there is a note, ask the family for permission to read it before they do. If the note is malicious, it may be better if they don't see the note, and remember their loved ones the way they were, not the way they were presented in the suicide note. If the family insists on reading it, share with them the person was not in a right state of mind. They may have been in a heightened emotional state, and wrote some things they really didn't mean.

There are many support groups available for those who have lost a loved one to suicide. When the time is right, it is very appropriate to make referrals to these support groups to help the bereaved move through their grief. The Chaplain should follow up with the family, and if so desired, help with funeral arrangements, and referrals for counseling.

I say again, there is no substitute for good training. I strongly recommend all chaplains get training in suicide prevention, intervention, and post-vention.

CHAPTER 16
OFFICER INVOLVED SHOOTINGS AND OFFICER DOWN CALLS

The young warrior, weary from battle and with his head hung low, sat on his horse. He was returning to his tribe. His shirt was covered in blood. It had been a hard fought, vicious, battle. There were many casualties on both sides. Some of his friends were among the slain. He had fought braves of the enemy tribe, and watched them die. This was the first time he had ever killed another human being. He and his companions had defended their families from the attacking marauders, and had driven them away. But he had mixed feelings. On one hand he felt proud for having the courage go into battle and do his duty, but on the other, he felt spent, ashamed and guilty for killing other men.

The Navajo warriors were welcomed back, but were not allowed back in to the camp. They would have to remain on the outskirts until they went through a cleansing ceremony. The members of their tribe would not call their names, or even look them in the eyes before the "Enemy Way" had been performed. They knew that war was difficult on them, and made it impossible for them to live in the ordinary, everyday world. The returning warriors needed to have their balance restored before they went to be with their families again. The tribe would practice their rituals to cleanse these returning war veterans of the effects of death and bring them some healing before being assimilated back into the tribe.

Most Indian tribes had traditions after a war, including telling their battle stories in words, songs and in other ways. Some used sand painting. Many used dance to rid them of the evil of battle. War veterans were held in high esteem, and most tribes believed they held special wisdom from having been part of battle.

At the writing of this book, the war in Iraq is drawing to a conclusion. Many of the returning veterans are "weekend warriors" as part of the National Guard or Reserve units. Many of these veterans are also law enforcement officers. They may have stories to tell, and certainly have had many experiences that they would never have chosen to go through. The native Indians knew the importance of ritual, storytelling, and giving time to their returning warriors. At the same time, their warriors understood the importance of letting the tribe help them heal physically, mentally, and spiritually. They embraced the rituals as a way of dealing with the horrors they had experienced.

Senator Bob Dole wrote the Foreword in a book called, "Courage After Fire." He says in the Foreword, "Coming back from war is a longer journey than any plane flight home. It would be great if everything just snapped back together the way it had always been – and if what happened in Tikrit stayed in Tikrit, for instance - but the truth is, returning from war is much more complicated than that. Digesting what you saw and what you missed and relating to your old world can be tough, even with terrific support. It feels unfair, considering the personal sacrifice. But fair or unfair, returning home is rarely what you imagine it will be." (15)

When a LEO experiences an officer involved shooting; responds to a horrific scene; or experiences the worst that our society has to offer – just as our returning warriors – there are things that get on us that "we just can't wash off". It's not an act of courage to shove our emotions down and not deal with what happened. Many officers will go to the bar to deal with it. Having "Choir Practice" at the bar is not the most effective way to deal with what they have gone through. Self medicating in these circumstances is never a good idea, whether they use alcohol, sugar, or other substances. It takes doing something to cleanse the effects of death. Encouraging them to tell their story to a safe person such as the Chaplain can be the start of that healing.

Part of the Navajo warrior tradition was the willingness to engage the enemy in battle. The qualities of a warrior included strength, honor, pride, devotion and wisdom. These same qualities and tradition can be found in our modern day warriors. Those who have sworn an oath to serve and protect have shown not only the willingness, but the courage to face whatever comes each day. But the Navajo warriors also knew they needed each other and they knew when to seek the support of the tribe.

The conclusion of Senator Dole's forward in "Courage After Fire" is very poignant in pointing out true courage. I don't think I could put it any better. It reads: "In battle, courage means sacrificing our own well-being for fellow soldiers and for our country. After battle, courage means concentrating on and being honest with ourselves, using all the tools we can gather to lead the best life we can, and, by example, giving something to those who will follow in our footsteps." (16)

A law enforcement officer will experience critical incidents. If they are in this career field long enough they will see death. They may find themselves in a position where they have to take a life, and they will very likely know someone who does. They are told this from the time they are in academy. It is part of the calling of being in law enforcement.

When they do experience a critical incident, they need to be prepared. They need to not hesitate to embrace their own rituals; seek strength from their spiritual side and get support from their own faith community. They should be encouraged to talk to the Chaplain and get support. This will help build their resilience. Above all, they should be to taught to know themselves, and know when they need to have the courage to seek help from a safe person, and then not put it off.

The most impacting type of calls on a department and individual officers will be those that involve shooting and killing a suspect, and those involving an officer down. These calls will involve a lot of time and work on the part of the Chaplain.

According to statistics, law enforcement officers kill between 300 and 350 people in the line of duty every year. The statistics also show that there are 600 to 700 such line of duty shootings every year. That means about 30% of those people shot by law enforcement officers will suffer fatal wounds, and die. As a Chaplain, you will very likely be called out on officer involved shootings, so you need to be prepared, and aware of what is going to happen, and what you can do to help. (17)

Traditionally, law enforcement officers have accepted officer involved shootings as part of the job, and have tried to swallow their raw emotions along with an excess of alcohol (choir practice). Naturally, this tendency has lead law enforcement officers to become hard and cynical. This is something we are trying to prevent from happening.

As with other critical incidents, the officer may feel a rush of different emotions, or they may feel numb, and not feel anything at all. This is normal, and it needs to be explained to them that what they are feeling is normal. Over the course of the next few days, they will probably play the scene over and over in their heads, and have a gauntlet of different feelings and emotions.

Most officers tend to go to one extreme or the other when one of their own shoots and kills a suspect. They will either avoid the person, because they don't know what to say, and don't want to say the wrong thing; or they will make it out like it is a big joke, and say something totally inappropriate like "Hey Killer!" The Chaplain needs to explain how to treat the officer, and what they may experience when dealing with partners and other officers from the same shift, and even different shifts. One of the best things the fellow officers can do for their co-worker who has been involved in a shooting is to ask them how they are doing, and then tell them, "I'm really glad that YOU are o.k." This will bring comfort to the officer, make them feel accepted, and that he is not ostracized for doing the job he or she is paid to do. When you talk with the officer involved in a shooting, always listen to their story first, and find out "where they are", then share.

The officer that kills a suspect may begin to ask questions. One of the most common, even for those officers that are not particularly religious, is what about "Thou shalt not kill"? Lt. Col Dave Grossman, the author of "On Killing", does an excellent job of explaining this issue in his seminars. He walks through the Bible starting with Exodus 20:13 where the commandment of not killing first appears. He shows how the word "kill" in Exodus 20:13, is actually better translated "murder". So it says, "Thou shalt not murder." He then goes on and talks about how in 1 Samuel 18:7 as a soldier, "David killed his tens of thousands": how in II Chronicles 18:6 it says "The Lord gave victory to David": and in II Samuel chapter 11, David's troubles all began when he "murdered" Uriah. In Proverbs 6:17 the Bible says God hates "shedders of innocent blood". Grossman lists out several other passages, including how the 1st gentile Christian in the Bible was Cornelius a Centurion (our equivalent today would be the police officer, or soldier). (18)

When an officer is involved in a shooting incident, depending on the situation he or she may report having different perceptual distortions. About 85% of those involved in a shooting will experience diminished hearing. They may not hear the report from their weapon. They may get tunnel vision. Time may seem to move in slow motion, to the point that they feel like they are paralyzed. One sense may take over, while their other senses fade away. (19) It has been shown scientifically that these are all survival instincts that kick in. An example may be an officer going into a dark room, and being shot at. All of a sudden, their eyesight may go away leading to temporary blindness, but their hearing will become heightened. In another scenario they may see a person shooting at them. Their hearing may go away temporarily. They may not be able to hear the shots, but their vision may become super human. The senses that are the most important when their life is suddenly in danger will often times take over. Explaining this to an officer will often help them know they are not going "crazy".

Anytime you have an officer involved shooting, it becomes an "all hands on deck" event. You will want to have Chaplains go to the scene; to the stationhouse; and to dispatch if there are enough available. All of these people will need a Chaplain. The presence of a Chaplain will often be enough to bring re-assurance and calm. In most cases, the officer(s) who did the shooting will have their weapon taken from them for forensic testing. In the best-case scenarios, they will immediately be given a replacement weapon. They will then be taken "downtown" or to the station house for interviewing by the detectives. The Chaplain should go with the officer, but not ask about the shooting at this time. Just be there to reassure them, and let them know the process of what will be taking place. Even if they are aware of the process, it is comforting and reassuring to explain it to them again. You may also want to get permission from the detective in charge and the officer to call his or her spouse, or have them call to reassure their family that they are O.K.

While the shooting officer is being interviewed, try to be a servant to the other officers at hand, and any family members that happen to show up. Fix coffee; get cold water, or whatever is needed. It is a good idea that the officers involved in the shooting not drive themselves home. Either help to arrange a ride for the officer, or offer to drive them home yourself.

Officer Down:

Police work is a dangerous occupation, and there are times when officers may be injured on the job. They may be attacked by criminals, and stabbed or shot; they may have motor vehicle crashes; or a host of other injury causing incidents. I have been on calls where an officer was mistakenly attacked by a police dog; have had heart attacks while on duty; have had an aneurysm; and various calls for broken limbs, or cuts and bruises from being in fights or car crashes. Often times, officers will be injured while off duty, or their family members may be hurt. I was once asked to respond to a call where a high-speed pursuit ended up in a suspect crashing his car through the bedroom wall of an officer's daughter. She was at home, but fortunately she was not in her bed when the car went over it. These kinds of calls should be taken just as seriously as those involving officers on duty.

Of course not all officers die in the line of duty. Cancer, heart attacks, and other physical ailments take the lives of many officers. In many cases, the officer may not die immediately or quickly e.g. a terminal cancer diagnosis.

Ministering to those that are dying and the family members of the terminally ill can be very complicated. There are many demands placed on the Chaplain. The Chaplain must be caring and compassionate, but also knowledgeable and able to pass on their knowledge to the patient and their family.

There are a few points to be aware of when dealing with the terminally ill. To be effective in ministry to the dying, the Chaplain must first know where they stand personally, spiritually, and theologically on death. Ignorance, and fear in this area will severely handicap the ability of the Chaplain to minister in these situations. It is vital at times like this that the Chaplain not only be a spiritual person (many religions that don't even believe in God claim to be spiritual), but have a real faith in a genuine God. In most cases, this will be not only assumed, but also expected.

The question of what to tell a dying person may come up to the Chaplain; i.e. should the dying person be told that they are dying. I can think of no exceptions when the truth should not be told to the dying person. They have the right to know the truth, and will appreciate your honesty much more than you're not wanting to "hurt them". The result can be devastating if the person is not told they are dying, they somehow survive, and later discover they were not told the truth. The Chaplain's "philosophy" about death will make it much easier to talk with the dying person. Even if the person doesn't consider themselves religious, it can be pointed out that nature itself shows an example of life after death. Even a seed has to fall to the ground and die, in order to come back to a new life. Natural science has shown that energy never disappears, but merely changes from one form to another. Of course Christianity, along with most all religions, point to the opportunity of the re-unification with God after death. Dying people would rather have some hope to cling onto, that death is not the end. After all, if there is no consciousness after death, what is there to fear?

The dying patient, even a big "tough" officer, will very likely have a degree of fear of death. It is often a fear of the unknown. "We all become frightened when threatened by a danger with which we are unable to cope or control effectively. The "unknown" in physical death is related to the ambiguousness of the future. The individual fantasizes the worst possible outcome and reacts to the threat of this anticipated hopeless, overwhelming danger. The dying person's denial is a means of avoiding the need to face this anxiety provoking state of the future. Institutions and the professionals representing those situations are supposed to have the appropriate answers. When one has an answer that is definitive, then one is relieved of the need to project what is often the most negative outcome." (20)

Elisabeth Kubler-Ross MD, a psychiatrist, wrote a ground breaking book called "On Death and Dying" in 1969. Her definitive work described the typical reactions and patterns a person goes through in the process of dying. Basically, these steps or patterns go in this order:

1. Denial
2. Anger
3. Bargaining
4. Depression
5. Resignation (as opposed to acceptance)

Most every dying person will go through these different phases. They may not always come in order; the person may move forward and backward through the phases; they may get stuck for a longer period of time in one of the phases; and they may experience more than one phase at a time. Giving the dying person and the family members the knowledge of these phases will help ease much of their discomfort, and help them realize they are normal.

What you attempt to do with a dying person needs to depend on them, and where they are. The Chaplain needs to carefully evaluate body language, and how a person is doing physically. They may be too physically exhausted or in too much pain to really benefit from your being there. Be sensitive to this, and minister to them at their level. Encourage them to be very open and honest with you, and to tell you if they are not up for a visit, or if you are thinking of leaving and they really want you to stay longer.

Aside from compassion and knowledge, there are a few other things that will be required of the Chaplain ministering to the dying. "Patience is needed to let the dying person struggle with pain and mortality while the minister waits to be invited to contribute and share. Strength is required to help another wage a losing battle with death. Insight is necessary to see the patient's changing needs, feelings, and thoughts. And love! Only love can make the other three possible. Our first and final goal must be simply to love the dying person." (21) And in the still quiet moments, when we give all we have to give, ""his gift born of dedicated service allows us to experience the glory of God's grace as He embraces both the living and the dying. It is as close as many of us will ever come during our time on earth to touching the face of God." (22)

The Chaplain should be preparing the family of the dying person for the transition following the death of their loved one. The family will likely suffer through anticipatory grief. "It is as real and painful as that which occurs after death and requires the same caring ministry." (23) Anticipatory grief, if managed well by the Chaplain, can help lower the intensity of grief suffered after the death of their loved one. The Chaplain needs to be available to the family and loved ones as well as to the dying patient during this time. Work with family members to make funeral arrangements, and any other final arrangements. This can be done with the help of the dying person. It will help bring reality of the impending death to all involved. "When death finally comes, it triggers severe emotional stress. The deep pain fostered by the realization that the deceased is permanently lost to them now rushes in, and the comfort of the minister is never more needed or appreciated." (24)

Sometimes the very worst happens, and an officer will be killed in the line of duty. A line of duty death has a rippling effect that will very likely have an effect on the entire state, and sometimes even into neighboring states. The men and women in law enforcement "experience a grief that few civilians truly understand. A line of duty death impacts the agency or department to its very core." (25) The big picture is there will be a huge funeral service, likely including hundreds if not thousands of officers from the department, and even some from several hundred miles away. The camaraderie among law enforcement officers runs very deep -- officers will come from far and near to honor, and pay their respect to their fallen comrades. It is important to coordinate all aspects of the funeral, including contact with and placement of the media. As you look at the medium sized picture, there is a department, a shift, and a team of officers that have lost one of their own, and are feeling hurt, and devastated. Perhaps the dispatcher who got the initial call, "officer down" is feeling guilty, as if he or she could have done something more. And finally, as we draw the picture even tighter, we see a family that has lost a spouse, a mom or dad, a brother or sister, and a son or daughter. All of these elements or pictures if you will, must be worked with, without ignoring any of the three. This takes a great deal of coordination and work, and it may be advisable to seek the assistance of other Chaplains from other jurisdictions.

We can pray, and hope that we never have to deal with a line of duty death, but the reality is that we probably will. And, since that is the case, the Chaplain should make every effort to be prepared for this eventuality before it happens – there needs to be a plan already in place.

Every department will be a little bit different, but every department should have a policy in place on how to deal with an officer's line of duty death. If your department does not have one, it is highly recommended that you sit down with the heads of your department and discuss putting together a policy before you need one. It should include some of the following:

1.   A phone list of who to call immediately following a line of duty death. This should include the Chief or Sheriff, and the Chaplain.

2.   Who will notify the family? Normally, this will be the Chaplain escorted by a high-ranking official(s) in the department.

3.   After the family has been notified, who else will be notified? Heads of departments – dispatch – media – etc. All should be done in a timely manner, and with as much tact, respecting the privacy of the family, as possible

4.   Consider the implications of the officers that knew the deceased, and hear about it from another source, such as the media, instead of through the department. There should be a procedure in place to have all off duty personnel called in such a situation.

5.   There will be a need for a facility to house a very large funeral. A large local Church is usually the best options, but there may be other options such as halls or lodges in your area.

6.   Formal debriefing with the Chaplain; presence at briefings for all shifts; dispatch; and family.

7.   What will be included in the funeral service –
such things as honor guard, who will speak at the funeral,
media presence, fly-overs, bagpipes, uniformed officers,
final salute, seating for family and officers, security issues,
public dignitaries such as from the governors or mayor's
office, etc.

8.   Many of the same things in point number seven
need to be considered for the graveside service as well.

9.   Reception for the family and friends. The heads
of the department and the Chaplain should be in
attendance at these functions as well.

10.   There will be different policies on non-line of duty
deaths, such as suicides, after retirement, deaths during
vacations, or simply off duty deaths.

11.   Try to think of any contingencies not covered,
and get them all down on paper so everyone will be on the
same page.

No matter what the cause of death for the officer,
remember the deceased was still a "fellow officer" and the
survivors will always be part of the "police family". Even if
it wasn't a line of duty death, encourage the officers to be
there.   If it was a line of duty death, encourage the
department to get coverage from other departments at
least for those officers that worked the same shift. I have
seen cases where an entire department covered for another
department while they all attended the funeral for a very
popular fallen officer.
    In concluding this book, it comes to mind that no matter
how prepared you are, or how much you know, every call is
going to be different. As you do the work of the Chaplain,
be vigilant, and prayerful. You never know what comment
you may say, or it may even be just your presence that will
make the difference in an officer's life. Whether it be going

on a ride along or just passing the time; attending a retirement party for a long time officer or conducting a wedding or a funeral, your presence will be appreciated. You will be missed when you are not there as God gives you inroads into the lives of these noble people called law enforcement officers.

As a Law Enforcement Chaplain, you are about to begin one of the most challenging, yet most rewarding ministries you can do. In light of that, I would like to take the opportunity to pray for every person who reads this:

Dear Heavenly Father,

Even as the disciples in the book of Acts in the New Testament were prayed for and sent out into the world to minister, we pray for these new chaplains. We pray that your anointing would be upon them to do this work you have called them to, and that you would cause them to be effective in the Chaplain ministry.

As these chaplains go forth to minister to people at the most tragic and most vulnerable times of their lives, we pray that you would help them to exhort and counsel the emotionally wounded. Help them to bring peace and calm to situations where all about them the storms of life are raging.

Help these chaplains to be good and effective listeners. Help them to share the pain of those they are called to; and gently lead them to healing, and restoration. Help them to use wisdom and give them insight when to speak and what to say.

Father establish these your chaplains with strength, honesty and conviction as they go forth representing you to a hurting world. Give them your Holy Spirit to guide them.

Help these chaplains to never stop growing in you, but to continue to mature, as they seek your face.

We ask these things in your name,

Amen

OTHER BOOKS BY THIS AUTHOR

"Life Celebrations – a Guide for Funeral and Memorial Services"

A practical how to book on funerals and memorials.

"What to do when Grief Kidnaps Your Soul"

A book on grief in all of its faces.

"The Church Chaplain's Role-Meeting the Need in the Church and Community"

Picks up where the Chaplain's Role left off, giving practical instruction for church chaplain/compassion ministries.

"Starting with God – a Guide for New Believers"

A little book to help new Christians with their first steps into their new found walk with Jesus.

APPENDIX A

Sources for additional help and Information

1. International Conference of Police Chaplains (ICPC)

Offering training, various courses, and general help with chaplain programs

(850) 654-9736

www.icpc4cops.org

2. International Critical Incident Stress Foundation (ICISF)
Training in Critical Incident Stress Management

Emergency number (410) 313-2473

Regular phone (410) 750-9600

www.icisf.org

3. Gold Country Chaplaincy
Offering training, general help with Chaplain programs, and one to one counsel

(916) 936-1962

www.goldcountrychaplaincy.org

goldcountryadmin@gmail.com

4. Trinity Biblical University
Offering courses and degree programs in Law Enforcement Chaplaincy

(707) 438-0703

www.tbu.edu

5. Army One Source
Help for all military (all branches) and their families on a variety of issues. On line courses in working with military veterans.

http://www.myarmyonesource.com

6. Police USA/Chaplains USA
(Excellent source of training and assistance with Line of Duty Death Funerals. John Cooley Seminars – can be contacted through the website.)

http://www.policeusa.com/

7. Living Works
Provides ASIST (Applied Suicide intervention Skills Training) suicide intervention courses. Excellent training.

NOTES TO SECTION I

(1) Romans 13:1-6, Living Bible

(2) On Killing, by Lt. Col. Dave Grossman, Published by Little, Brown and Company: Page 183

(3) IBID Page 183 and 184

(4) The Epistle of Paul to the Romans, by F. F. Bruce, Published by Tyndale Press, Copyright 1963, page 238, and quoting, A. R. Vidler, Christ's Strange Work, 1944, Page 28.

(5) From the Law Enforcement Chaplaincy Sacramento – Law Enforcement Chaplain Academy III, class hand outs, Chaplain Mindi Russell, April 1999

(6) Information on the selection process of a police officer taken from the San Diego Police Dept. Web site

(7) Code of Chivalry from "The Code of Chivalry" web site

(8) Information about the Paladins taken from "The Paladin" web site, MSN Encarta, and "The Complete Paladin's Handbook" by Rick Swan, TSR Ltd. 1994.

(9) FBI Law Enforcement Bulletin – December 1, 1973

(10) Webster's II New Riverside Dictionary, Houghton Mifflin Co, Copyright 1996

(11) Concepts for the transition from Altruism to Cynicism from, Law Enforcement Chaplaincy - Sacramento – Community Chaplain Academy IV, March 97, class entitled "Law Enforcement Profession/Philosophy" taught by Chaplain Mark O'Sullivan

(12) Webster's II New Riverside Dictionary, Houghton Mifflin Co, Copyright 1996

(13) Critical Incidents: Debriefing and Immediate Aftercare, by Keith Bettinger. This article can be found at "tearsofacop.com"

(14) Critical Incident Stress Information Sheets, from the Critical Incident Stress Management basic course workbook, by Jeffrey T. Mitchell, Ph.D, C.T.S. and George S. Everly, Jr. PhD., F.A.P.M., C.T.S. 1998

(15)"Do Cops Really Like Donuts?"   by Glenn Norstrem, found at web site WWW.Merriam-park.org

(16)"Law Enforcement and the Police Family," Cassette Recording No. APA 95-081, Washington D.C., by R.P. Delprino, C.L. Kennedy, J. Cardarelli and C. Goss: American Psychological Association, 1995

(17) "Developing a Law Enforcement Stress Program for Officers and Their Families", Part of a series: NIJ Issues and Practices, Published: March 1997

(18) Information on sleep deprivation caused by shift work comes based on the article "Shift Work and Officer Survival", by Thomas J Aveni, a staff member of , The Police Policy Studies Council

(19) Taken from lecture notes from the lecture "On Killing" by Lt. Colonel Dave Grossman

(20) "Developing a Law Enforcement Stress Program for Officers and Their Families", Part of a series: NIJ Issues and Practices, Published: March 1997

(21) From an article by Diversity Central called "Rainbow & Blue: A Summary of Lesbian/Gay/Bisexual/Transgender issues in Law Enforcement" by Dr. Berenice Ruhl

(22) Quoted from the New International Version of the Bible

(23) Statistical data from "The Future of Women in Policing", by the International Association of Chiefs of Police, November, 1998

(24) "Not so Obvious Police Stress", by Terry Constant.   From the "Tears of a Cop" website, at WWW.tearsofacop.com

(25) Ibid

(26) "Police Officers and Compassion Fatigue" by Sgt. Steve Albrecht, San Diego Police Reserve

(27) Ibid

(28) "Police Officers and Compassion Fatigue" by Sgt. Steve Albrecht, San Diego Police Reserve

(29) Concepts for the psychological autopsy from, Law Enforcement Chaplaincy Sacramento – Community Chaplain Academy IV, March 97, class entitled "Chaplain's Philosophy" taught by Chaplain Mindi Russell

(30) "Ripples of Suicide", by Harold Elliott, with Brad Bailey, WRS Publishing, 1993 page 37

(31) Ibid

(32) "Critical Incident Stress Management basic course workbook", by Jeffrey T. Mitchell, Ph.D, C.T.S. and George S. Everly, Jr. PhD., F.A.P.M., C.T.S. 1998, pg 31

(33) "CopShock Surviving Posttraumatic stress Disorder (PTSD)" by Allen R. Kates, Holbrook Street Press, copyright 1999, page 56

(34) "Workers' Compensation for Law Enforcement Related Post Traumatic Stress Disorder", Behavioral Sciences and the Law, V8, 1990, pages 447-456 by J.P. Mann and J. Neece

(35) "Suicide by Cop: The Long Road Back", by Rebecca Stincelli, 1998-2001

(36) "Crisis Intervention: Suicide in Progress – A Working Document", by Barry Perrou, Psy.D., Public Research Institute, 1999, as quoted in an article entitled "Suicide by Cop Results of Current Empirical Studies, by Louise C. Pyers, MS, Consultant – Community Psychology

(37) "Crisis Intervention: Suicide in Progress – A Working Document", by Barry Perrou, Psy.D., Public Research Institute, 1999

(38) "Suicide cops: in the line of duty" by Dateline NBC, 2000, as printed on the website WWW.tearsofacop.com

(39) Sacramento Bee newspaper article, "Kidnap Suspect Thanked Cops Who Shot Him", by Andy Furillo, 2/8/00

(40)Ibid

(41)"Suicide by Cop When it happens to you, there's almost always police stress as a result", by Hal Brown LICSW, 1998, revised 2003

(42) "Little Psychological Help for Officers", by Dateline NBC, 2000, as printed on the website WWW.tearsofacop.com

(43) "Critical Incidents: Debriefing and Immediate Aftercare" by Keith Bettinger, 2001, as printed on the website WWW.tearsofacop.com

(44) "American Police Hall of Fame", from the website WWW.aphf.org

(45) "Grieving Behind the Badge Emotional Support for Line of Duty Death Survivors", by Peggy Sweeney Rainone, 1998

(46) Ibid

(47) "Words that can Change Your Life Forever", by Dwight A. Polk, MSW, NREM-P

(48) "Developing a Law Enforcement Stress Program for Officers and Their Families", Series NIJ Issues and Practices, March 1997

(49) "Mass Media and Law Enforcement – A Time for Reflection", by Edward J. Tully from the National Executive Institute Associates, Major Cities Chiefs Associations and Major County Sheriff's Association

(50) Ibid

(51) Ibid

(52) "What are the Uniquely Stressful Aspects of Policing", by Michael Babin, RCMP Gazette, 1983

(53) "Mass Media and Law Enforcement – A Time for Reflection", by Edward J. Tully from the National Executive

Institute Associates, Major Cities Chiefs Associations and Major County Sheriff's Association

(54) "What are the Uniquely Stressful Aspects of Policing", by Michael Babin, RCMP Gazette, 1983

(55) "Why do police officers have such an outlandish rate of marital and domestic failure and calamity?" By Police Chief Chuck Pratt (Retired), author of Police Headquarters

(56) Ibid

(57) "The Effects of Stress on Police Officers", by Dan Goldfarb, Ph.D., a law enforcement officer counselor in Long Island since 1984, taken from a speech given to a group of Police Union delegates

(58) Ibid

NOTES TO SECTION II

(1) Jeremiah 10:5, from the New International Version of the Bible, Zondervan Bible Publishers, 1985

(2) "Developing a Law Enforcement Stress Program for Officers and Their Families", Part of a series: NIJ Issues and Practices, Published: March 1997

(3) Ibid

(4) "10 Reasons Cops are Different and How These Differences Impact on their Stress", by Daniel A. Goldfarb, Ph.D. from the website www.heavybadge.com

(5) "Not so Obvious Police Stress", by Terry Constant. From the "Tears of a Cop" website, at WWW.tearsofacop.com

(6) "Parlay International' 1995

(7) Ibid

(8) Ibid

(9) "Heros Among Heros" by Mark Smith, from the website www.heavybadge.com

(10) "Critical Incident Stress Management: The Basic Course Workbook," by Jeffrey T. Mitchell, Ph.D, C.T.S. and George S. Everly, Jr. PhD. F.A.P.M., C.T.S. 1998, page 31

(11) Ibid

(12) Ibid

(13) "American Family Physician" A Peer Journal for the American Academy of Family Physicians, December 15th, 2003. "Diagnosis and Management of Post-traumatic Stress Disorder" by Bradley D. Grinage, M.D.

(14) "Turning Points: Treating Families in Transition and Crisis" by Frank S. Pittman III, New York: Norton, 1987, Chapter 7, "Infidelity: The Secret Insanity"

(15) "Christian Counseling a Comprehensive Guide", by Gary R. Collins, Ph.D., Word Publishing, 1988, page 454

(16) Concepts for the major causes of divorce taken from, "Christian Counseling a Comprehensive Guide", by Gary R. Collins, Ph.D., Word Publishing, 1988 chapter 30

(17) "Developing a Law Enforcement Stress Program for Officers and Their Families", Part of a series: NIJ Issues and Practices, Published: March 1997

(18) Information regarding suicide survey came from handouts from Law Enforcement Chaplaincy Sacramento – Law Enforcement Chaplain Academy III, May, 1999; class entitled "Police Suicide Awareness" taught by Chaplain Mindi Russell

(19) "Suicide" by the Central Florida Police Stress Unit, Inc. From the website www.policestress.org

(20) "Police Suicide: Hidden Epidemic Across the Country", by Jules Loh, The Orlando Sentinel, January 30th, 1994, as quoting Cindy Goss, certified counselor for drug and alcohol abuse, in Erie County NY.

NOTES TO SECTION III

(1) Proverbs 27:17, from the New International Version of the Bible, Zondervan Bible Publishers, 1985

(2) Acts 27:20, from the New International Version of the Bible, Zondervan Bible Publishers, 1985

(3) "Developing a Law Enforcement Stress Program for Officers and Their Families", Series NIJ Issues and Practices, March 1997

(4) I Corinthians 9:19, from the New International Version of the Bible, Zondervan Bible Publishers, 1985

(5) "Developing a Law Enforcement Stress Program for Officers and Their Families", Series NIJ Issues and Practices, March 1997

(6) I Corinthians 9:22, from the New International Version of the Bible, Zondervan Bible Publishers, 1985

(7) "Developing a Law Enforcement Stress Program for Officers and Their Families", Series NIJ Issues and Practices, March 1997

(8) Concepts for qualifications for a law enforcement chaplain from Law Enforcement Chaplaincy Sacramento – Community Chaplain Academy IV, March 97, class entitled "Law Enforcement Profession/Philosophy" taught by Chaplain Mark O'Sullivan

(9) "Developing a Law Enforcement Stress Program for Officers and Their Families",

Series NIJ Issues and Practices, March 1997

(10) "Talk of the Nation/Science Friday", April 25th, National Public Radio interview

With Radio Anchor Ira Flatow, quote made by Lieutenant Colonel Elspeth Cameron Ritchie, a psychiatrist for the Medical Corps and the program director for Mental Health Policy and Women's Issues in the Office of the Assistant Secretary of Defense for Health Affairs in the Department of Defense.

(11) "Developing a Law Enforcement Stress Program for Officers and Their Families", Series NIJ Issues and Practices, March 1997

(12) Ibid

(13) "Chaplain Ride-Alongs...Asset vs. Liability" by Rocklin Police Sergeant Rick Eaton, lecture notes from Law Enforcement Chaplaincy – Sacramento Training Academy, April 1999

(14) "Developing a Law Enforcement Stress Program for Officers and Their Families", Series NIJ Issues and Practices, March 1997

(15) First Amendment to the United States of America Constitution

(16) Lemon V.S. Kurtzman, U.S. Supreme Court Case 403 U.S. 602, 1971

(17) "Developing a Law Enforcement Stress Program for Officers and Their Families", Series NIJ Issues and Practices, March 1997

(18) Concepts came from lectures and notes from the Law Enforcement Chaplaincy Sacramento – Academy III, Chaplain Mindi Russell, "Marital and Family Issues Specific to Law Enforcement Personnel" April, 1999

(19) "Developing a Law Enforcement Stress Program for Officers and Their Families", Series NIJ Issues and Practices, March 1997

(20) "Cop Shock", by Allen R. Kates, Holbrook Street Press, 1999

NOTES TO SECTION IV

(1) Matthew 14:22-32, from the New International Version of the Bible, Zondervan Bible Publishers, 1985

(2) "Police Chaplains Serve a Special Need", by Laureen Fagan, South Bend IN, Tribune Staff writer, 7/12/01

(3) "Good Men and Women Really Do Cry", By Chaplain Jerry Montgomery, NorthWest Region ICPC newsletter, June 2000

(4) Ibid

(5) Ibid

(6) "Not so Obvious Police Stress", by Terry Constant, from the website www.tearsofacop.com

(7) Ibid

(8) "The Home Front Marital and Family Issues Specific to Law Enforcement Personnel"

(9) Marital Counseling goals concepts from "Christian Counseling", by Gary R. Collins, Ph.D., Word Publishing, 1988

(10) "Developing a Law Enforcement Stress Program for Officers and Their Families", Series NIJ Issues and Practices, March 1997

(11) "Ripples of Suicide", by Harold Elliott with Brad Bailey, page 150, WRS Publishing, 1993

(12) Concepts for Suicide Scale of Lethality from Law Enforcement Chaplain Academy IV, April 1997, lecture and hand-out by Chaplain Mindi Russell

(13) "Ripples of Suicide", by Harold Elliott with Brad Bailey, page 117, WRS Publishing, 1993

(14) Ibid, page 133

(15) "Courage After Fire", by Keith Armstrong, L.C.S.W., Suzanne Best, Ph.D., and Paula Domenici, Ph.D., Foreword by Senator Bob Dole, pages 1-3, Ulysses Press

(16) Ibid

(17) Concepts for Suicide intervention from Law Enforcement Chaplain Academy IV, April 1997, lecture and hand-out by Chaplain Mindi Russell

(18) Statistics of killings and shootings Law Enforcement Chaplain Academy III, May 1999, lecture by Chaplain Mindi Russell

(19) Presentation on Killology, by Lt. Colonel Dave Grossman, 2000

(20) Ibid

(21) "Resources for Ministry in Death and Dying", by Larry A. Platt, and Roger G. Branch, Broadman Press, 1988, page 122

(22) Ibid, page 141

(23) Ibid, page 141

(24) Ibid, page 154

(25) Ibid, page 155

(26) "Grieving Behind the Badge, Emotional Support for Line of Duty Death Survivors", by Peggy Sweeney Rainone, from the website www.geocities.com

.

BIBLIOGRAPHY

(1)"American Police Hall of Fame", from the website WWW.aphf.org

(2)"Chaplain Ride-Alongs...Asset vs. Liability" by Rocklin Police Sergeant Rick Eaton, lecture notes from Law Enforcement Chaplaincy – Sacramento Training Academy 1999

(3)"Christian Counseling a Comprehensive Guide", by Gary R. Collins, Ph.D., Word Publishing, 1988

(4)"Christ's Strange Work", by A. R. Vidler, 1944

(5)"Code of Chivalry, The" web site

(6)"Complete Paladin's Handbook, The" by Rick Swan, TSR Ltd. 1994.

(7)"CopShock Surviving Posttraumatic stress Disorder (PTSD)" by Allen R. Kates, Holbrook Street Press, copyright 1999

(8)"Courage After Fire", by Keith Armstrong, L.C.S.W., Suzanne Best, Ph.D., and Paula Domenici, Ph.D., Ulysses Press, copyright 2006

(9)"Crisis Intervention: Suicide in Progress – A Working Document", by Barry Perrou, Psy.D., Public Research Institute, 1999,

(10)"Critical Incidents: Debriefing and Immediate Aftercare" by Keith Bettinger, 2001, as printed on the website WWW.tearsofacop.com

(11) Critical Incident Stress Management basic course workbook, by Jeffrey T. Mitchell, Ph.D, C.T.S. and George S. Everly, Jr. PhD., F.A.P.M., C.T.S. 1998

(12) "Developing a Law Enforcement Stress Program for Officers and Their Families", Part of a series: NIJ Issues and Practices, Published: March 1997

(13) "Do Cops Really Like Donuts?" by Glenn Norstrem

(14) "Effects of Stress on Police Officers, The", by Dan Goldfarb, Ph.D., a law enforcement officer counselor in Long Island since 1984, taken from a speech given to a group of Police Union delegates

(15) "Epistle of Paul to the Romans, The", by F. F. Bruce, Published by Tyndale Press, Copyright 1963

(16) FBI Law Enforcement Bulletin – December 1, 1973

(17) First Amendment to the United States of America Constitution

(18) "Future of Women in Policing, The", by the International Association of Chiefs of Police, November, 1998

(19) "Good Men and Women Really Do Cry", By Chaplain Jerry Montgomery, NorthWest Region ICPC newsletter, June 2000

(20) "Grieving Behind the Badge Emotional Support for Line of Duty Death Survivors", by Peggy Sweeney Rainone, 1998

(21) "Heroes Among Heroes" by Mark Smith, from the website www.heavybadge.com

(22) "Home Front Marital and Family Issues Specific to Law Enforcement Personnel, The"

(23) "Kidnap Suspect Thanked Cops Who Shot Him", by Andy Furillo, Sacramento Bee newspaper article 2/8/00

(24) "Killology", seminar presentation by Lt. Colonel Dave Grossman, 2000

(25) "Law Enforcement and the Police Family," Cassette Recording No. APA 95-081, Washington D.C.,

by R.P. Delprino, C.L. Kennedy, J. Cardarelli and C. Goss: American Psychological Association, 1995

(26) Law Enforcement Chaplaincy Sacramento – Academies, and lecture notes, various instructors including but not limited to Chaplains Frank Russell, Mindi Russell, and Phil Whitbeck, and officers from various departments

(27) Lemon V.S. Kurtzman, U.S. Supreme Court Case 403 U.S. 602, 1971

(28) "Little Psychological Help for Officers", by Dateline NBC, 2000, as printed on the website WWW.tearsofacop.com

(29) Living Bible

(30) Living Works – ASIST Suicide intervention training.   More information can be found at www.**livingworks**.net/.

(31) "Mass Media and Law Enforcement – A Time for Reflection", by Edward J. Tully from the National Executive Institute Associates, Major Cities Chiefs Associations and Major County Sheriff's Association

(32) "MSN Encarta"

(33) New International Version of the Bible

(34) "Not so Obvious Police Stress", by Terry Constant.   From the "Tears of a Cop" website, at WWW.tearsofacop.com

(35) On Killing, by Lt. Col. Dave Grossman, Published by Little, Brown and Company:

(36) "Paladin, The" web site

(37) "Parlay International' 1995

(38) "Police Chaplains Serve a Special Need", by Laureen Fagan, South Bend IN, Tribune Staff writer, 7/12/01

(39) "Police Officers and Compassion Fatigue" by Sgt. Steve Albrecht, San Diego Police Reserve

(40) "Police Suicide: Hidden Epidemic Across the Country", by Jules Loh, The Orlando Sentinel, January 30th, 1994, as quoting Cindy Goss, certified counselor for drug and alcohol abuse, in Erie County NY.

(41) Police USA and John Cooley training seminars on Line of Duty Death Funerals.   More information at www.**policeusa**.com/

(42) "Rainbow & Blue: A Summary of Lesbian/Gay/Bisexual/Transgender   issues   in   Law Enforcement" by Dr. Berenice Ruhl

(43) "Resources for Ministry in Death and Dying", by Larry A. Platt, and Roger G. Branch, Broadman Press, 1988, page 122

(44) "Ripples of Suicide", by Harold Elliott, with Brad Bailey, WRS Publishing, 1993

(45) San Diego Police Dept. Web site

(46) "Shift Work and Officer Survival", by Thomas J Aveni, a staff member of , The Police Policy Studies Council

(47) "Suicide" by the Central Florida Police Stress Unit, Inc. From the website www.policestress.org

(48) "Suicide by Cop Results of Current Empirical Studies, by Louise C. Pyers, MS, Consultant – Community Psychology

(49) "Suicide by Cop: The Long Road Back", by Rebecca Stincelli, 1998-2001

(50) "Suicide by Cop When it happens to you, there's almost always police stress as a result", by Hal Brown LICSW, 1998, revised 2003

(51) "Suicide cops: in the line of duty" by Dateline NBC,   2000,   as   printed   on   the   website WWW.tearsofacop.com

(52) "Talk of the Nation/Science Friday", April 25th, National Public Radio interview with Radio Anchor Ira Flatow, quote made by Lieutenant Colonel Elspeth Cameron Ritchie, a psychiatrist for the Medical Corps and the program director for Mental Health Policy and Women's Issues in the Office of the Assistant Secretary of Defense for Health Affairs in the Department of Defense.

(53) "Turning Points: Treating Families in Transition and Crisis" by Frank S. Pittman III, New York: Norton, 1987

(54) Webster's II New Riverside Dictionary, Houghton Mifflin Co, Copyright 1996

(55) "What are the Uniquely Stressful Aspects of Policing", by Michael Babin, RCMP Gazette, 1983

(56) "Why do police officers have such an outlandish rate of marital and domestic failure and calamity?" by Police Chief Chuck Pratt (Retired), author of Police Headquarters

(57) "Words that can Change Your Life Forever", by Dwight A. Polk, MSW, NREM-P

(58) "Workers' Compensation for Law Enforcement Related Post Traumatic Stress Disorder", Behavioral Sciences and the Law, V8, 1990, by J.P. Mann and J. Neece

(59) "10 Reasons Cops are Different and How These Differences Impact on their Stress", by Daniel A. Goldfarb, Ph.D. from the website www.heavybadge.com

-

Chaplain Terry Morgan

198

ABOUT THE AUTHOR

Chaplain **Terry Morgan** is an ordained minister with over 30 years of experience. He has spent over 20 years as a law enforcement chaplain. He is currently the Pastor of the Church of the Indwelling in Redding, CA, and the Senior Chaplain/Executive Director of Gold Country Chaplaincy and Press4hope. Morgan attained the Master Chaplain Level of the International Conference of Police Chaplains, and is a member of the International Critical Incident Stress Foundation. He received his Board Certification in Emergency Crisis Response through the American Academy of Experts in Traumatic Stress. Chaplain Morgan has extensive training, and is a certified trainer for QPR suicide prevention, and a provisional trainer for ASIST suicide intervention. He is a member in good standing with the "Assn. of the United States Army" (AUSA). Chaplain Morgan has sat on several boards representing the Faith based Community including the boards of the "Campaign for Community Wellness," and "Advocates for the Mentally Ill Housing". He is the past President of the Board for the Gold Country Veteran Stand Down. Most recently he became a Local Board Member for the Selective Service System Region III and a Board Member of the national organization, "PoliceUSA".

Chaplain Morgan was one of a handful of law enforcement chaplains chosen to work with Louisiana Mental Health and the New Orleans Police Dept. immediately following Hurricane Katrina. He has also been one of only a few chaplains selected to work with surviving family members of officers killed in the line *of duty during "National Police Week" in Washington D.C.*

Chaplain Morgan earned his Masters degree in Ministry in Public Safety, from Trinity Biblical University and his Bachelors degree in Theology from Pacific Coast Bible College. He also has an Associate of Science Degree in Business Management from Sacramento City College. He has taught Bible college courses, and teaches crisis counseling for chaplains. He is often called upon as an expert in dealing with traumatic stress, and stress management. He has been frequently published in Officer.com magazine on a variety of topics related to law enforcement, and has been featured in "PORAC" magazine and "Extant Magazine". He has written numerous articles for several local newspapers, including the Auburn Journal as a guest contributor. He is the author of the books "The Chaplain's Role, How Clergy Can Work With Law Enforcement", "Life Celebrations a Guide for Funeral and Memorial Services", "What to do When Grief Kidnaps Your Soul" and "Starting With God". His first book "The Chaplain's Role", was recently picked up by Liberty University as a textbook for their chaplain course "CHPL 598 Chaplain Formation Practicum". Chaplain Morgan teaches various ministries how to help their own parishioners through critical incidents, crisis, moral injury, and traumatic events, while exercising good stress management techniques and preventing compassion fatigue or burn out in their ministers.

Chaplain Morgan can be reached by email at chaplainmorgan@gmail.com, or by phone at 916-936-1962